Please Return:
Qwana & Preston

ISBN: 978-1-61061-851-9

www.GetAndStayMotivated.com

GET OFF YOUR 'BUT' &
MAKE IT HAPPEN!

A "NO EXCUSES"
BLUEPRINT
FOR MAKING YOUR
NEXT BIG MOVE
AND CREATING A
'KICK-BUT'
CAREER AND LIFE!

Jonathan Sprinkles

To:_____

From: _____

"I hated every minute of training, but I said, 'Don't quit.
Suffer now and live the rest of your life as a champion.'"
-Muhammad Ali

DEDICATION

To Jaxson.

You are going to change the world.
You inspire me.

TABLE OF CONTENTS

FINDING THE COURAGE TO PURSUE YOUR PASSION

In May of 2002, I sat at my desk at work, staring into a blank computer screen. It was like I was watching myself on television. I literally saw a vision of me standing before a large audience of people, delivering a rousing message. All of a sudden, I had a headache; and it wasn't because my headset was too tight.

Clearly, I was out of place and I knew it.

I was on the fast track to management. I was known as one of the top sales reps. I was making over $80,000 only two years removed from college. But it wasn't what I was supposed to be doing with my life.

While I should have been paying attention in a meeting one day, I had a moment of inspiration and scribbled down the words "your 'BUT' is too big!"

It became the title and premise for an essay I wrote about how many excuses we make instead of doing something to fix problems. I loved the piece, but even more so, I loved the process. I got lost in time, finding creative ways to stretch this play on words to get my point across. I got excited and cracked a smile every time I thought about how this article was going to get people thinking differently. I was in love and couldn't shake it.

I started talking to kids on weekends about staying in school and making positive choices. Admittedly, I was more noise than I was substance, but my love grew deeper nevertheless.

Not long after, I quit.

Many years, thousands of lives touched, and quite a few books later, I still haven't looked back.

Just FYI, I make a lot of assumptions about you in this book. I assume that you bought, borrowed, or stole this book because you want something. You are in pursuit of something greater and you're ready for a change. If so, great. The hungrier you are, the more you'll appreciate my tell-it-like-it-is style and tone. I am not a guy who spends lots of time placating you with motivational puffery. You picked up this book because you wanted one thing—results. And I want to help you get them.

This book is to serve as your daily guide and kick in the rear. Sort of like a GPS with an attitude. I was originally going to title the book simply "Make It Happen," one of my favorite phrases to use with my coaching clients. But for some reason, that title never sat well with me for this project. I needed something that was indicative of my true feelings about the inverse relationship between excuses and success. Finally, when I was asked to provide guest commentary on a national television program about the large numbers of people who are blaming the economy, politicians, and everybody else but themselves for their woes, I hit my breaking point. I had enough. Sitting in front of the camera, going through my notes one last time before the show, the catchy phrase from my essay years prior reemerged. Under my breath, I muttered, "Y'all (with my Texas accent) need to get off your 'BUT' and make it happen."

I was fed up with the foolishness. The same year unemployment grew to a record high, Americans bought 714 million dollars of ringtones for their cell phones. The same folks who are complaining that the guy in the oval office can't provide jobs for them are turning away from books, but buying cell phone apps, sporting designer handbags, and overdosing on up to four hours a day of television.

Whatever happened to having a dream, starting off dead broke, working your tail off, making extreme sacrifices, and becoming a mega success because of it?

Nowadays, if anyone is "crazy" enough to do this, it becomes a national headline. People tell them, "Whoa, you ought to have your own reality show!" What?

Our minds are saturated with entertainment, entitlement, and instant gratification. We are losing that inner fortitude and self-determination that causes us to defy the odds, break through our barriers, and change the game forever. We are acquiescing too much and fighting too little. We are spending more time on our couches and virtually no time at the library or hustling on our grind. As a result, obesity has become the leading cause of preventable death worldwide. Our "I want it my way or not at all" attitude is literally killing us. As our 'BUTS' are growing, our butts are too.

Getting off your 'BUT' isn't an option. It is mandatory for you if you are going to enjoy living your purpose and avoid wasting your talents. There has never been a better time in history for people who are courageous enough to believe in themselves, put in the work, and make it happen. While others are slacking off, you step up. It's yours for the taking!

As of today, I am kicking you out of the nest. With love, of course.

If you're still teetering between wimping out and going after what's in your heart, consider these truths:

- **Someone's wanting**–You are going to help a lot of people when you step out on faith. Just seeing you show up will encourage someone.
- **Someone's waiting**–There is someone right now who would hire you. They're looking for you. They would be excited about making you a celebrated member of their team. You have to first let go of what you have to get what you want!
- **Someone's wishing**–Someone is hoping you don't take advantage the next time the window of opportunity opens. They will happily take your spot. The void will be filled, with you or without you.

Make no mistake. Being brave enough to step out into the unknown where there are no guarantees takes a lot of guts. Anyone who has done it but denies being scared witless is lying. I sure was. But I studied the habits of the most successful people and discovered that those who make it big share some common characteristics. Focus on these traits for yourself and watch how quickly your confidence, concentration, and preparedness to take the big risk will rise:

- **Attitude**–You have to believe in your vision despite what you may see with your eyes.
- **Associations**–You are who you hang around. Find someone who has the level of success that you want and shadow them. Learn their habits and replicate them.
- **Actions**–Your habits will determine your career. Be the hardest worker you know. Do the extra work that nobody else is willing to do and you'll get what nobody else is able to have.
- **Accountability**–Put yourself out there. Tell 10 people about your plans to pursue your passion. Don't say, "I want to so-and-so," say "I am doing it." Write positive affirmations beginning with the words I AM and post them around your house. Don't just set a goal; become it.

Choose to succeed, no matter what it takes. Most people are willing to "give it a shot," but you have to be willing to keep shooting until you hit your target. This time, it's different. This time, you win.

Congratulations in advance,

JONATHAN SPRINKLES

HOW TO USE THIS BOOK

G*et Off Your 'BUT' and Make it Happen* was not written to be a novel. Don't approach this as one of those "one and done" books. Believe it or not, it took me a long time to create this book, so it should take you a while to fully "get" what I'm saying.

This book wasn't written; it was accumulated. Over the course of several years, little jewels of wisdom were deposited in me as I sought to overcome challenges I went through. Some I shared with my social media community. Others, I kept private, waiting for a special occasion, such as this.

In order to get the most from our time together, I suggest you go one step beyond simply reading this book and setting it down. To experience it in its fullness, make it a part of your daily ritual.

Here are some ideas:

1. Write your favorite sayings down, commit them to memory, and use them in your conversations.
2. Post quotes on your social media pages.
3. Add quotes to your email signature and periodically rotate them so people will be curious to read your latest dose of inspiration. (This is a trick to get people to actually read all your emails.)
4. Write timely quotes on index cards or sticky notes and put them around your office.
5. Write a "quote of the week" on your meeting agenda. Ask everyone to comment on what it means to them.
6. Write your favorite quotes on sheets of colored paper, cut them out individually, put them in a clear glass jar, and give it to someone you would like to encourage. Label it "In Case of Emergency."
7. Give this book to colleagues, subordinates, and clients as an appreciation gift.
8. Read this book with your family. Use the themes as discussion topics.
9. Write your favorite quotes on your mirror with an erasable marker to energize and focus you for the day.
10. Comment on the book on YouTube. Be sure to tag the book as a keyword, so you can get "free traffic" when your video comes up as a related video to the others who have also tagged it.

Get Off Your 'BUT' And **BUILD YOUR CONFIDENCE**

"In order to go from where you are to where you want to be, you have to grow from how you are to how you ought to be."

-Jonathan Sprinkles

Because we are just getting to know each other, I'll start things off by revealing a little bit about myself.

I want to be in great shape and muscular—no, ripped—but I struggle to work out consistently. I am a very passionate person—to a fault. When I am working on a big project, I can get so engrossed in my work, it consumes the bulk of my attention. I will sometimes wake up (after only a few hours of sleeping on my couch), head to my office, start up my computer, and get busy. The next time I pick my head up for air, it's already afternoon. These days are bittersweet. Although I have gotten a lot of items checked off my list—which is a feeling I love—I often neglect the basics, such as eating and exercising. This isn't always the case; but when it happens, I feel it.

A favorite pastime of mine, one that affords me the opportunity to bring balance to my life, get clarity in my thoughts, and stay in shape, is running. Some of my best ideas have come on the trail. I have 30 or so minutes to

12

myself, unimpeded by calls, emails, and text messages. It is *my time*.

As much as I love the sport, I'm still no speedster. It is not uncommon to see me getting passed by white-haired men with short shorts, pulled up socks, and running shoes with Velcro fasteners. Hey, those guys can move! Anyhow, the point is, I enjoy the activity, but I'm not going to challenge for any records. A few years ago, I ran a personal best time around the three-mile trail at Rice University in 23 minutes, 15 seconds. In my mind, I was smoking! That was my Boston Marathon. As I sprinted across the finish line with my arms raised, I felt my inner Kenyan come out. I sent a mass text to all my friends, bragging, and even thanking God for blessing me with such swift feet. One of my friends, a Warrant Officer in the US Army, was kind enough to reply to my text, informing me that my record time would have been respectable even by military standards—if I were a female.

You get the point.

I never realized how much about running is mental. Your mind gives out long before your body does. Marathoners are familiar with the term "hitting the wall," which is the moment in every race when your body wants to shut down, and only your sheer determination to keep going allows you to continue on. Film superstar, Will Smith, once shared some pearls of wisdom on this topic at a *Teen Choice Awards* ceremony. When you run, he explained, there is always a "little man" who shows up and whispers in your ear, encouraging you to quit. He reminds you how tired you are and how much you're hurting. Will said that if you can learn how to keep that man quiet, you will always cross the finish line in your race and in life. Although during a race, you see runners staring at their watches, trying to beat the clock, the real quest is to out-will that little man. Those who can defeat him are the ones you see achieving amazing times. Those who can't are the ones you see pulled over on the side, grabbing their shorts, gasping for air.

I didn't like to run long distances for this reason. There was no little man on my shoulder. He was more like a sumo wrestler on my back! In high school, we only had to run one mile for class. For years, that was all I ever attempted. It wasn't until my senior year in college that I dared venture beyond that distance. Of course, there was a girl involved. I was invited to run one evening with a friend of mine. The problem was, her daily routine was two miles long. Although we were just platonic friends, my ego still wasn't going to let me stop short and have her laugh at me. Although I had no clue what would happen next, after I reached one mile I kept going. I "let her" keep a healthy lead in front of me so she couldn't see me wheezing, whining, and whimpering behind her. I was totally gassed; but miraculously, I finished. The next morning, my legs were so stiff, I tried to get out of bed and fell on the floor!

Two miles became my new limit. Then, a few years later, I was invited to do a "Thanksgiving Turkey Trot" 5K race. That was 3.125 miles! Of course, it was a girl who invited me. And of course, I accepted.

I'll never forget that race. It was freezing cold. I wore two layers of clothes. I couldn't feel my toes. When the race began, my chivalrous ways kicked in once again, and I "allowed" her to keep a lead ahead of me. I justified my slow pace by convincing myself that I was saving myself for a burst at the end. But when a woman pushing her twins in a stroller passed me, I was highly offended. I sped up. My ears were covered, so I could hear my deep breaths and my chest pounding. The sumo wrestler started whispering something to me in Japanese that sounded like "take a cab home!" If I hadn't left my wallet in the car, I swear I would have. But when I looked down, I discovered something that gave me an instant boost of energy. Spray painted on the street were orange mile markers that allowed us to see our progress and calculate the remaining distance. Sweet!

I challenged myself to just hit the next mile marker;

then I could decide if I needed to take a break. I made a game of it, going from marker to marker, gaining energy from seeing the number of kilometers to completion shrink. As I neared the final turn, I saw a marker that said, "400 meters." I remembered that was the distance of one lap around a track. I sprinted. However, what I failed to realize was how freakin' far 400 meters is when your legs feel like rubber.

Again, I was wheezing, whining, and whimpering. As I ran, my jaw dropped so far, my bottom lip was nearly hitting my chest. I saw a mile marker that said, "300 meters." At this point, the mile markers had betrayed me, so I closed my eyes and went for it. I figured that when I opened my eyes, I should've been at the finish line. With eyes shut tightly, I sprinted for, what felt like five minutes. I opened my eyes, looked down, and saw another mile marker—"290 meters."

I finished the race, but I was beat up. I think my time may have been respectable for the wheelchair division. On the way home, I almost ripped down a sign that explained that there was also a 10K for "serious runners" that was being held concurrently. The 5K was nicknamed the "Fun Run." There wasn't anything *fun* about it!

Many great lessons can be extracted from running. I appreciate how the sport makes you a better person after every outing. Personally, what has been most useful for my business and my life has been my new friend from the "Fun Run"—the mile markers.

Achieving any goal, be it losing 40 pounds, increasing your grade point average, making more money, or cleaning out your life, is just like a race. It takes a long time to complete, the finish line is nowhere in sight for the majority of the journey, and you are always tempted to pull over and take a break or quit altogether. Fortunately, the same tools that inspire you to finish a race are also useful for getting you to an outcome you have been hoping for.

On your personal journey, you will need mile markers to help you gage your improvement along the way. These are commonly referred to as benchmarks, milestones, or critical success indicators. The names vary, but their function is the same.

1. Mile markers reflect your progress.

This is essential to achieving your goals without losing your motivation along the way. Remember, the majority of the race is mental. It feels good to know how far you have come. This is why personal trainers encourage you to take a notebook with you to the gym and record the number of reps you did and the weight you used. Your growth is evident when you see both numbers steadily increase week by week. This is why smart managers display the names of everyone on their team on a board, lining them up like horses at the starting gate of the Kentucky Derby or racecars at the Indy 500. They move a name forward when the person achieves an important milestone that puts them closer to the key initiative. Not only does this create an undeniable snapshot of who is handling their business, it infuses the competitive juices of the entire team.

Progress is a strong motivator in and of itself. Seeing where you are compared to where you were is often reason enough to keep going. Even though you may not be "there" yet, you certainly are better than you were when you began. A couple who argues three times a week has reason to be proud if they make note of the fact that they used to argue six times a week. As the old folks would say, "We're not all we're 'sposed to be, but thank God we're not what we used to be."

2. Mile markers measure your pace.

You have heard me say it before, and I'll say it a thousand more times, "If you can't measure it, you can't manage it." A goal without a gage is incomplete. The reason why most people fall short of obtaining their desired outcome is because they fail to chop the large number into smaller coefficients that are bite-sized and less intimidating. Losing 40 pounds is a daunting task, but losing two pounds a week for 20 weeks doesn't sound so bad. Heck, the first five pounds will come off when you stop drinking soft drinks. The point is, breaking down your goal along a timeline punctuated by periodic "mini deadlines" empowers you to have a frame of reference for your progress. You can take the most direct sequence of actions instead of hoping that everything will somehow work out in the end. **Mile markers convert "hope" into strategy.** Adding daily, weekly, or monthly timetables to your plan enables you to know with certainty, "by this time, I should be here," hence taking the guesswork out of the process. This is great because you have immediate feedback about where you stand in relation to where you should be.

> **Mile markers convert "hope" into strategy.**

Mile markers also give you a reason to celebrate along the way. This is yet another strategy for staying focused, but it is overlooked by nearly everyone. It's a brilliant tool. Think about it; you aren't going to invite people to your "10 Pounds Off" party, then scarf down a cheeseburger that evening. When you "go public" about your goal, you put yourself out there and have a greater level of accountability because you know how much it's going to suck if you have to tell them that you fell off. In this instance, peer pressure is a very good thing.

3. Mile markers intensify your momentum.

When I got to the end of the race, I didn't care about the cold air stinging my face or the burning sensation going up and down my legs. I was so close, and all I could picture was crossing the finish line. Without thinking about it, I found a burst of energy I didn't know I had. Watching the distance remaining numbers decrease as I ran was such a motivating factor that by the time I got to a place I felt like I could easily handle it, I bolted. This is what mile markers do for you. They make you more aggressive and competitive, even when you are competing against yourself. They provide recurring doses of "you can do this" and encourage you to finish strong.

As a young salesman, I would listen to audiotapes (yes, tapes!) on my drive to and from work. I enjoyed listening to sales gurus teach about the nuances of selling, from the clothes you should wear to how to address people so you build instant rapport and how to ask for the sale with confidence. The lesson that stuck with me the longest, however, was about the mindset a salesman should have. Because we are all human, even the most confident among us have areas of self-doubt. To a salesman, these insecurities, when projected toward the prospect, can keep you from closing the deal. Master sales trainer Brian Tracy was responsible for teaching me one of my most valuable lessons about how to keep insecurities from getting the best of me. "Do you know when the best time is to ask for a sale?" he asked. "Just after you made a sale." He explained that the first thing we should do after signing the papers to close one deal is pick up the phone and ask another prospect for their business. As you ride the high of one deal, you forget about your fear of rejection and go all out toward reaching your next pinnacle.

> ## The more you win, the more you crave winning.

Success breeds more success. Robert Cialdini, author of the powerful classic *Influence: The psychology of persuasion*, explains, "Once a stand is taken, there is a natural tendency to behave in ways that are stubbornly consistent with the stand." Completing one conversation that you've been putting off builds momentum toward having another. Cooking one great meal whets your appetite for getting back in the kitchen and doing it again and again. Losing the first seven pounds makes you anxious to see how quickly you can shed the remaining ten.

One unique strategy I have on goal attainment is being intentional about how you begin. Always start strong. Build your momentum by purposefully creating a string of small victories in the beginning to grow your confidence. What these victories are doesn't matter. They can be as simple as drinking eight glasses of water a day, walking around the block, checking your mailbox, or reading one article in your favorite magazine. The next day, you integrate a more substantive goal, then another, until you have eased your way into the fast lane, already possessing a winning record. The initial phase is 100 percent about getting the ball rolling in the right direction. It is essential that, from the start, you achieve your goals (no matter how small), and subsequently view yourself as making progress. You must feel successful. **The more you win, the more you crave winning.** The little triumphs along the way will boost your self-confidence and will intensify your passion to get to the big victory in the end.

4. Mile markers build your confidence.

The greatest of all benefits that mile markers bring is the confidence that you develop because of them. As your momentum builds, so does your confidence. Both your self-talk and your self-image change. You go from saying, "I want XYZ" to saying, "I deserve it, and will put in the work until I get it." Striving strengthens you. Making the daily decision to forsake your excuses and stay on your grind makes you feel like a better person. It gives you something to be proud of and a future to protect. As coach Vince Lombardi said, "The harder you work, the harder it is to quit."

Most importantly, you develop a sense of accomplishment that, when internalized, can effectuate change in other areas of your life. When you achieve the impossible in one area, you start to believe in yourself more and seek to apply your newfound power toward achieving other goals. You say to yourself, "Now that I've done this, I can do anything."

In everything you do, confidence is key. I have taught for years that you will never outperform your own self-image. The way you see yourself is who you will become. If you have a Clear Mental Picture of yourself getting a degree, becoming the Team Lead, owning your own business, or having a firm physique, you will achieve it. You will, subconsciously, gravitate toward choices that will make it so. Beware; this principle goes both ways. If you have a Clear Mental Picture of being divorced, stuttering through your presentation, forgetting the answers to the test, or tiring out before the finish line, that's what you will achieve. Your confidence originates from this picture, which is created by your internal dialogue. What you say to yourself about yourself is the greatest factor in your success or failure.

Unfortunately, the majority of us aren't saying the right things to ourselves. If you interviewed ten random people on the street, eight out of the ten would attest to being critical or even negative toward themselves. You can't succeed like this. **Your words, your beliefs, and your results, in time, will become one.** You will notice, I frequently talk about your internal conversation. This is why. Winners don't go around saying, "I hope I don't lose." They don't beat themselves up. They are hard on themselves, but not harsh. We know not to be too cruel toward children because it may impact their self-esteem and kill their confidence. What makes you think the rules change when you're talking to yourself?

> **Your words, your beliefs, and your results, in time, will become one.**

Confident people make different choices than those who lack confidence. They don't complain; they get creative. They don't let themselves get easily depressed; they become determined. Confident people don't settle for what feels best; they make the tough decision to do what feels right. They say, "If it is going to be, it is up to me!" When confident people fall off the horse, they don't get up and smack the horse. They just learn to ride better!

I know both sides of the confidence spectrum now. Whatever level of self-assurance I have now, I was equally as timid for the majority of my life. I went to several different school systems as a result of my parents' divorce. Starting in each new school, always being the new kid or the only black kid in class, I hated being different. I used conformity as my coping mechanism. I adapted to the dominant culture in every environment.

Unknowingly, I decayed my self-esteem because the conversation I had within was, "I am not good enough as I am, so I have to change in order to be accepted." As a result, I learned to become a "character" rather than my true self. I often remained quiet, hoping not to be "found out" if I talked too much. Surprisingly, I am still an introvert today.

Most people don't believe me when I tell them this, especially if they first met me at an event where they saw my onstage persona. I am very high-energy on stage, but reserved everywhere else. It confuses those who want to put me in a box and label me as one specific type of person. I am frequently asked, "Which side is really you?" Both! I know how to "turn up the volume" when necessary; but I am most comfortable in an intimate space. Don't get me wrong; I am an introvert, not socially inept! I am comfortable in a crowded room; but I am most confident when I am at my best, helping someone one-on-one.

In which setting(s) do you feel most confident?

_____

_____

_____

_____

I used to beat myself up about my introversion. I used to think there was something wrong with me. However, I came to discover that I was in good company. There is a long list of well-known high achievers who are also quiet, shy, or introverted. Here is a partial list of some notable names:

Neil Armstrong – Astronaut, first man to walk on
the moon
Lucille Ball – Actor
Robert De Niro – Actor
Thomas Edison – Inventor

Ulysses S. Grant – Civil War General, US President
Robert Frost – Author, poet
Tom Hanks – Actor
David Letterman – Comedian, television host
Abraham Lincoln – US President
Brad Pitt – Actor
Elvis Presley – Singer
Joan Rivers – Comedian
Ben Stiller – Actor

I was stunned to see some of the people on the list. It even forced me, an introvert, to reexamine my stereotype of introverts. It is clear, however, that there is no correlation between quietness and confidence. You don't have to be the life of the party or have a dominant personality in order to be successful. All you have to do is find what you're good at and be the best *you* that you can be.

Where Your Self-Image Comes From

Experience
"How you compared yourself to people in the past."

Existence
"How you believe people view you compared to your peers right now."

Expectations
"How your potential compares to that of your peers."

What qualities (physical or mental) make you stand out from others?

_____

_____

_____

_____

What do you often become self-conscious about?

_____

_____

_____

How does your future compare with that of your peer group?

_____

_____

_____

_____

What Makes You Hot?

I attend a lot of conferences annually. As a speaker, it is fun and rewarding to meet new people and spread my message. Nevertheless, things can become a little monotonous at times. One day, I decided to stir things up. About 30 minutes prior to my breakout session, I carried the flip chart from the front and stuck it two feet outside my room.

I grabbed a marker with the boldest color I could find and wrote "Sexy Black Man" with an arrow pointing down the center aisle toward the platform. When people filed into the hall, the rumble of laugher became progressively louder. In retrospect, I don't know if they were laughing because of what the sign said or laughing because it referred to me. It created such a buzz, I stuck with it, and have kept it as part of every presentation.

The truth is, I really don't consider myself sexy. Silly? Yes. Corny? Oh yeah. Sexy? Not so much. There are sexy people in this world, but I'm not one of them. I'm okay with that. I know I am a very nice guy, and even a decent looking guy. No woman would hear her friends say, "Girl, I guess the pickings were slim when you chose him," when she introduced me to her people. A little notoriety in my career and a few dashes of success have made people occasionally look at me differently. But not me. I know what's up. When I go to the mall in Houston, Los Angeles, Miami, or New York, nobody breaks their neck to get a second glimpse. I don't get approached by gawking women who are taken aback by such a beautiful man. If that did ever happen, I would wonder what was wrong with them. When I'm just being me, blending into the crowd, I'm rated as "aiight," definitely not sexy.

I use the "Sexy Black Man" joke because, well, it's funny. Beyond that, it represents a monumental step for me, the skinny kid with a big head and acne who couldn't get a date with a pocket full of 50 dollar bills, to be at peace with himself enough to even go there. Years ago, I needed so much validation, I wouldn't dare bring up the topic because I couldn't take hearing the customary "below-average" feedback. Because that's how I grew up, my appearance now plays only a small factor in my self-confidence. I have developed other parts of my personality that cause me to stand up straighter and stick my chest out. If I were to consider myself sexy, it would be attributed to something you would have to know about me, not something you could see on me. But it all began with my first having the courage to say it, unapologetically, until I became more comfortable with the topic.

Boxing champion Muhammad Ali (at the time known as a young Cassius Clay), made a name for himself as a young man by boasting before and after each fight. He was legendary for his showboating. He would look in the camera and say, "I'm pretty! I'm pretty! I'm a baaaaad man!" When I visited The Muhammad Ali Center in his hometown, Louisville, Kentucky, I learned about a side of him I didn't know. It turns out he was so loud and boastful because he was not only trying to psych out his opponent, but also psych himself up. It was all bravado. One of his famous quotes written on the back wall of one of the classrooms summed it up, "I am the greatest. I said it before I knew I was."

Keep speaking who you want to be, in public and in your quiet time. Say it, even when there is no evidence of it yet. Say it…even before you believe it.

MAKE IT HAPPEN!

In what ways would having increased confidence improve your life? What would you do more of or ask for that you currently don't?

_____

_____

_____

List five times in your life when you felt most confident.

1. _____

2. _____

3. _____

4. _____

5. _____

List three internal self-talk statements you have made that lowered your confidence.

1. _____

2. _____

3. _____

IDEAS AND ACTION ITEMS

_____

_____

_____

_____

_____

_____

_____

_____

_____

_____

_____

_____

IDEAS AND ACTION ITEMS

Get Off Your 'BUT' And **GET YOUR ATTITUDE RIGHT**

"Our values are best reflected by our to-do lists. Where we spend our time reflects what is most important."

-Jonathan Sprinkles

Although there are times of year that are considered "goal-setting season," research emphatically suggests that you are statistically more likely to abandon your plans than you are to actually see the fruition of your dreams. Wow. Based on this conclusion, is it wiser to give up before you get started? Not so fast. This is the case for some, but it doesn't have to be the case for YOU. You have a right to claim whatever you work for. However, you may be working...too hard.

Please allow me to explain.

Because you're a smart person and a hard worker, you should expect your efforts to yield a positive outcome. You will almost always receive high marks, make lots of money, and have people tell you how great you're doing. This shouldn't surprise or impress you. You should expect it. This is great from a productivity perspective. But when the question shifts from "are you being productive" to "are you walking in your purpose," your measuring stick changes. **You should graduate from seeking to do what appeals to your esteem and instead seek to fulfill the calling on your life.** Instead of asking, "How much am I getting paid?" you should start asking, "Am I being obedient?"

> **You should graduate from seeking to do what appeals to your esteem and instead seek to fulfill the calling on your life.**

Think about both the places and people with whom you are currently spending a lot of your time. For example, start with your job and the five people with whom you spend most time. Answer the following questions:

- Do I feel at peace about being here, even when things aren't going as planned, or do I question my decision?

_____

_____

- Do I feel this job or relationship accelerates me toward my life's purpose or distracts me from it?

_____

_____

- If there were no consequences for changing my mind, would I make the same decision to be a part of this again?

_____

_____

You see, there is a big difference between doing something well and being where you're supposed to be. Based on intelligence alone, anyone can go to law school, but if you were supposed to be using your skills in another arena, you would consistently encounter what I call "divine discontent." Nothing will ever *fully* satisfy you, no matter how many awards, big paychecks, or outward symbols of success you earn. **Satisfaction comes only to those who are doing what they know they were put here to do.**

Life provides no lasting fulfillment outside of your purpose. But when you find it, embrace it, and walk in it, life provides no greater joy. This is what *New York Times* bestselling author Garrett Gunderson refers to as your "Soul Purpose." It the confluence of your vocation, your relationships, and your contribution to society all being in alignment with each other. This is where you get your sense of fulfillment or "feeling full" each day.

If you find yourself questioning your decisions or struggling with feelings of doubt and uncertainty about whether a person, a job, or a choice you made was a good fit, it probably isn't. These are all a byproduct of trying to "force it" to work. These thoughts don't arise when you have a natural fit. Challenges will always arise; but when you are in a situation

> **The longer you choose to dwell outside of the place you were meant to be, the longer you deny yourself the joy that you were meant to have.**

that feels right intuitively, you accept them as a temporary season, not a symbol of having made the wrong choice. **The longer you choose to dwell outside of the place you were meant to be, the longer you deny yourself the joy that you were meant to have.** No matter how good your life is, it gets better — much better — and more rewarding when you are living your Soul Purpose.

The most common myth is that you can either make money or you can do what you love. We have been led to believe that in order to be successful, you have to compromise your happiness. I disagree. So does Kirbyjohn Caldwell, author of *The Gospel of Goodsuccess*. He teaches, "There are two important days in every person's life. The first is the day they were born. The second is the day they discover why they were born." It is that second day, the day you discover why you were born, that you discover your "effortless income streams." These income streams are represented by money you earn by doing what you truly love. Your work breezes by, you are freaking amazing at it, and you enjoy every minute of the process. The work energizes you, versus work that normally drains you. You look forward to the next opportunity to do it again, instead of dreading having to do it again.

My wise colleague and marketing mentor Adam Urbanski once taught me, "Jonathan, think about what you do best and what comes easiest to you and charge the most for it." It was counterintuitive, so I didn't understand why that which I could do with my eyes closed would be of premium value. But upon further review, his suggestion was brilliant. Think about it—if you know you rock at something, you can guarantee a superlative outcome. Therefore, there is no risk involved in requiring people to invest more to have it.

There is a lifestyle component involved as well. If you spend your days helping people (who can afford you) achieve a result that enhances their lives and businesses, doesn't that also enhance yours? Could you see yourself being a little more amped up about coming to work? If you're unsure because you have not yet experienced this, I'll tell you from personal knowledge—the answer is yes!

What gets you excited? Wait…not in *that* way! You know what I mean. What fires you up just by thinking about it? It doesn't have to be anything big or "deep." It just has to be authentic. For starters, fill in the blank of this statement:

My inner light shines brightest when I am

_____.

I got clarity about my Soul Purpose when I answered this question. I am clearly happiest and my light shines brightest when I am serving people, especially when I am teaching or writing. You may say it shines brightest when you are cooking, playing with children, reading, walking among nature, giving to charity, fixing up cars, painting, connecting with friends on social media, or playing your favorite sport. Once again, it doesn't have to be "deep" as long as you're being honest with yourself.

Once you have identified one activity that causes your inner light to shine, press rewind and do it again. Find a total of five events that really melt your butter.

1. _____

2. _____

3. _____

4. _____

5. _____

Congratulations! You have just arrived at an important place in your life. In the space above, you have just acknowledged your five greatest gifts. Yes, your gifts. You enjoy the above activities because you are good at them, and they provide a sense of fulfillment. This is how your gifts express themselves, in the truest desires of your heart. This is the reason why, although these activities may require work, it doesn't feel like labor to you. You don't mind studying, reading, practicing, getting coached, or even failing a few times because you love developing your craft and you feel you have a high potential in this area. You find yourself fully engaged, and time seems to fly by. Ideas just "come to you" without much struggle. What stresses other people out, you find rather easy. Coincidentally, your five gifts are also your five "effortless income streams."

> **Take your passion, solve their problem, and turn a huge profit!**

No, I'm not suggesting you quit today and have an instant career change. You do, however, have clarity about what you can do in addition to your main stream of income (aka-your current job) that will provide additional revenue and add infinitely more satisfaction to your life. You can both serve the world and make a boatload of extra money by following your passion and doing what you love.

If you love to travel, you can write a unique, kick-butt blog advising people where they should stay on their next vacation. Once you develop a following, you can pick up a sponsor who pays you to talk about using their product on the road. If you get joy from being around kids, you can babysit part-time or on weekends. If you get joy from cooking, you can prepare and sell home-cooked meals for large families or young professionals who barely have time to wait on the oven to heat up.

The possibilities are endless. **Take your passion, solve their problem, and turn a huge profit!** By the way, these are all business ideas that have already been proven to work, so don't discount yourself or the value of your gift. The perfect fit *for you* exists. It's out there; you just have to go get it.

Working Less And Achieving More

The easiest path to "effortless income streams" in any context, even your current occupation, is to find the assignments that best fit your temperament. I sincerely believe that, of those who aren't prospering, it isn't because they aren't working hard enough. Actually, they're probably working too hard. More specifically, they're probably working too hard at jobs they'll be good at, but never great. Or perhaps more importantly, jobs they aren't not passionate about.

Your "good" effort is probably good enough to impress those around you, but you know there was more in you had you applied yourself. You know the clear difference between work that is a check in the box and that which is the result of you devoting your heart and soul to it. One is acceptable or above average. The other is so masterful it seems divinely inspired.

You can fool them all day long, but you're fooling yourself if you believe your half-effort doesn't weigh on your self-esteem. Can you really be proud of yourself when you know you're withholding your best work?

I have created a brief work style grid for you to determine which roles provide the best fit for you at work and at home. The four work styles are as follows: Director, Energizer, Connector, and Stabilizer. Read below to discover your primary temperament and how it affects your approach toward work.

DIRECTORS excel in careers and assignments that provide:

- A sense of autonomy over your work environment
- Opportunities for advancement

- Challenges and intellectual stimulation
- Fast-paced workflow
- Leadership of other people

Such as:

- Entrepreneur
- Management
- Sales
- Politics
- Fundraising

Because:

You like to be in charge and you don't like being told "No." You are confident, cool under pressure, a conceptual thinker. You search for mental challenges and usually believe you're right. Power is important to you. Winning is important to you. You don't mind the burden of being in authority. It feels natural to you.

ENERGIZERS excel in careers and assignments that provide:

- New challenges
- Positive feedback and public recognition
- Frequent changes of pace and scenery
- Up-beat interaction with others
- Working in teams

Such as:

- Public relations
- Retail sales
- Media/Entertainment
- Negotiating

Because:

You love to be around people. You have a gift for getting people to like you and follow your ideas. Your love for variety and adventure causes you to turn boring situations into memorable events. You are impatient, so you live in the now, which means you make the most of every moment.

CONNECTORS excel in careers and assignments that provide:

- Connection with your coworkers and those you serve
- A sense of working toward a greater mission
- Harmony and support from coworkers
- Opportunities to express your natural creativity

Such as:

- Human resources
- Healthcare (i.e. Nursing, Physical Therapy)
- Non-profit organizations
- Education
- Customer service

Because:

You will work harder to help others in need than you do for yourself. You get joy from working behind the scenes and don't require much personal attention. As long as everyone is happy, you're happy.

STABILIZERS excel in careers and assignments that provide:

- A traditional environment with clearly-defined roles
- Service to others via fixing inefficiencies within a system
- Opportunities to help others reach their potential
- Coordination, analysis, or project management

Such as:

- Technology
- Finance/accounting
- Healthcare (i.e. Surgeon, Specialist)
- Attorney
- Franchise owner
- Law Enforcement

Because:

The details that stress others out turn you on. You enjoy finding flaws and fixing them so the product will be perfect. You live by the rules and enjoy creating systems for others to follow. You specialize in turning chaos into order.

Chances are, you probably identified with traits in several, if not all categories. This is normal. Studies show that less than 10 percent of people fit exclusively into one category. Most of us are a combination of all of them. However, the same research also explains that there are, customarily, two of the four temperaments with which we can most closely identify. Without having the luxury of taking an assessment, the key to making this information work for you is to identify your two dominant temperaments and examine how they manifest in different situations. For example, you may primarily be a Director but have Energizer tendencies. Or, you may primarily operate out of your Stabilizer at work because of the nature of your job, but your Connector is expressed in your interpersonal relationships. Your persona is dynamic. It is not set in stone. Your top two temperaments often flip-flop as you adapt to fit your context. On occasion, circumstances may require you to tone down one part and accentuate another.

Most importantly, pay close attention to the work that best fits your temperament. Hopefully, this exercise brings you clarity about why you excel in some tasks and underperform in others. You may find yourself struggling with being bored or disinterested. It isn't that you are unintelligent or incapable. It may be as simple as you are in a position that doesn't "fit" you. Find one that does. Seek opportunities to do as much of that work as often as possible. Your best results will come from these assignments.

At a glance

	DIRECTOR	ENERGIZER	CONNECTOR	STABILIZER
Esteemed By:	Creating Change	Recognition	Pleasing People	Being of Service
Appreciated For:	Visionary Ideas	Spontaneity	"Glue" of an Organization	Attention to Detail
Specialty:	Strategy	Energy	Relationships	Quality
Need Most:	Affirmation of Your Wisdom	Visible Results	Personal Acceptance	Appreciating Your Service
Work Preference:	Independent	Variety	Small Groups	Structured Environments

Once you know that you're in the right place for you, doing the right thing, you will develop a quiet confidence that radiates from your core. What is often mis-labeled as a big ego is usually high self-efficacy. The two are different. Your ego is what you project to others. Self-efficacy is your expectation of what you are and are not capable of achieving. The former can get you in trouble; the latter gets you paid. Self-efficacy is the substance behind your swagger. It empowers you to conquer any challenge, ace any course, or overcome any obstacle. It is the little voice inside you that says, "I expect to win. I expect a high score. I expect to be atop the list of candidates. Nobody will out-work me. Nobody will be more prepared than me. Period."

Your level of expectancy can come from many sources of pride, such as:

- Family pedigree—"I am a Browder. We know how to turn nothing into something."
- Ethnicity—"We Italians know how to throw down in the kitchen."
- Place of origin—"I am from Brownsville. We never run and never will."
- History of overcoming—"If I could beat cancer, I know I can finish this marathon."

These are examples of self-efficacy in its purest form. It is the internal dialogue that compels you toward acting in congruence with your self-image. This is who you really are to yourself and what you really expect out of your life. It is revealed in those rare moments when you put aside all of the BS, the façades, and the pretenses; and you honestly say to yourself, "Because I am _____, I deserve to have _____." Eventually, it happens.

Your self-efficacy is highest in the areas that come most effortlessly to you. When I am teaching, I feel I have the potential to become one of the best of all time. When I am calculating numbers, I feel like a first-grader. Ironically, even acknowledging that I am good at what I do is a major milestone for me. I never considered myself to be an intellectual. Not at all.

The American education system doesn't cater much to creative, right-brained thinkers. I always rocked in English, but sucked in mathematics. My grades and self-esteem reflected it. It wasn't until years later, when I really honed my craft of dialing-in and helping people to bring out their core message and package it that I realized I had anything of value to offer to the world. I remember being so excited when I realized I was actually smart, I called my mother. Excitedly, I told her, "Hey mom, guess what? I'm pretty smart. No, seriously! I think I'm a genius." She quickly responded, "Yeah Jon, you are a genius…just not academically." Wow, thanks for the affirmation, mom.

The point is, I know what I'm good at, and what I'm not good at. Thus, I have very high self-efficacy when I'm on stage, when I'm coaching, and when I'm teaching. I hold myself to very high standards. I scrutinize everything. Why? Because I know I can be great, but only if I push myself. I catch mistakes others overlook. I take seriously what others blow off. It all matters to me. I hold myself to a high standard because I have the skills to fix what's wrong.

Kirk Nugent shares this sentiment about the poetry he has been producing for 15 years. His philosophy about his stringent work ethic is very straightforward — "I don't practice until I get it right; I practice until I can't get it wrong!" This is what makes the great, great — self-efficacy.

And Here Come The Haters…

Don't expect everyone to be excited about your discovering your passion and pursuing it. It ain't gonna happen. Most people you encounter don't have a clue about what their purpose is, nor do they have a clue how to find it. Expect that people will question your decision to go against tradition and step out on faith. When people discourage you from following an idea, it is your choice whether or not you listen to them. Regardless of who the person is, my advice is always the same—**consider the source.** If the person is sharing with you their insights and lessons learned from having already walked the path in which you're headed, you'd be a fool not to get out your pen and notepad. But if the person has no personal credibility, no experience, and offers nothing more than their unproven ideas, you'd be a fool to listen to them. **People can't give you directions to a place they've never been themselves.** I find it amusing how some people have strong opinions and swear they know what they're talking about, but have no authority or proof to speak of. Don't tell me your theory; show me your results!

> **People can't give you directions to a place they've never been themselves.**

Everyone is entitled to have an opinion, but not everyone should be permitted to speak into your life. I have learned the hard way that allowing too many people to advise you will leave you confused, scared, and overwhelmed. I made the mistake of entertaining everyone who pulled me aside to school me about my situation. Sure, they were all concerned, but many weren't qualified. I felt I owed it to them to listen to their counsel because it was rude to shut someone down who was trying to help. Unfortunately, this created internal conflict for me because I found myself wanting to make everyone happy by using pieces of their advice. Instead of heading in one direction, I started one way, reversed, and headed down another. My focus shifted from achieving my goal to pleasing my advisers. I was unsuccessful at both. This is why entertainment industry pioneer Bill Cosby said, "I don't know what the key to success is, but I know the key to failure is trying to make everyone happy." You have to discern whose merits qualify them to counsel you and to whom you need to politely say, "I already have my team who is helping me find the right answer for me." It doesn't mean you don't love or appreciate certain people in your life, but they may not be eligible to help you...*in this area.*

I believe scenarios such as this inspired the phrase *it's lonely at the top.* Most people simply won't get what it's like to be you. They won't understand the intricacies and nuances of being a risk taker. They can't identify with being so obsessed with your craft. They don't understand why you're always "in your head," analyzing solutions and figuring out your next move. It doesn't make them bad people; you just live in different worlds. They have different temperaments and tolerance levels. Only others who face similar challenges will truly get it (usually without much explanation because they are going through the same experience themselves). For example, I just conducted a coaching call yesterday in which I was helping one of my clients overcome a challenge she was having in her new business. After a few buzzwords I picked up from her, I knew exactly where she was and how to get her unstuck. I told her, "You're struggling with this; you're frustrated with that; and because you aren't where you expected to be, now you're worried about ever achieving this over here. Right?"

"Jonathan, how did you just read my mind like that?" she asked. "It's like you were here with me when I was having this conversation just yesterday."

I assured her that I was not wiretapping her home. I could speak with specificity and accuracy about her situation as a new business owner because I have been there myself. I go through the same struggles and know very well how lonely it can be when it feels like nobody can help you get untangled. Much of the work, you have to do on your own. Supporters can love on you and tell you how great you are; but outside of making you feel better momentarily, it still doesn't solve anything. They mean well, but sometimes you need some answers they just don't have.

This explains why most high achievers keep very small circles. To illustrate this point, I once asked a panel I moderated consisting of celebrities, professional athletes, and high-level executives, to each reveal how many true friends they had. These were some of the top names in their industries, all of which you would easily recognize.

The highest was four. The lowest was one. One of them answered, "Kinda three…if you include my mom." Because of the panelists' status, everyone in the audience was shocked. I wasn't. However, I did raise my eyebrow when I learned that every decision pertaining to Hall of Fame basketball player Michael Jordan, his Jordan brand, and his business ventures flows through a team of only six people, including Michael. Considering that, even long after his retirement, his brand is still among the most recognized in the world, it speaks to how tight Michael keeps his inner circle. He has specific people who serve a specific purpose. Everyone else can wait outside the room until the verdicts have been rendered.

Michael Jordan obviously gets it. I hope you do, too. There is a time to be open and a time to stand your ground. Producer extraordinaire Quincy Jones met Ray Charles when they were 15-years-old. At the time, there were virtually no African American role models in the entertainment industry; only Count Basie and Duke Ellington. As two up-and-coming pioneers in the business, they had to become mentally tough if they were to survive their journey. As Quincy recounts, every day he and Ray would look at each other and say, "Not one drop of my self-worth is dependent on your acceptance of me." Then he really drove it home for me. He said, "You have to know who you are. You figure out who you are. *Don't let someone decide for you.*" I'll give you two guesses whether

Quincy's inner circle is large or small.

What this means for you is you have to develop the skill of being self-correcting because other than your coach or mentor (which you *must* get if you don't already have one), you won't have many people to lean on who can actually help you the way you need. It means you have to study your craft diligently, create a clear image of your best-case scenario, and identify a cadre of other people to whom you can compare yourself. Personally, I am a believer in collecting examples from historical greats within your industry. Knowing the history of where your industry has been gives you a profound understanding of where you are now and enables you to predict what is going to happen next. You never just want to be a talent; you want to be an expert. Talent frequently gets taken advantage of; experts get respect. You earn your respect by knowing the game inside-out. Thus, I rely heavily on my own self-analysis to spot flaws and shore up my weaknesses. There is a series of questions I ask myself as I review my performance in everything I do.

1. Was it the best that I could do?

I am very honest with myself. If I set the bar too low just to appease myself with a grade, I won't strive to become better. If I absolutely gave it my all and my performance was a reflection of that, I answer, "Yes" and examine what I did compared to what I should have done.

Side note: I very rarely believe I perform at my best. There is always room for improvement. Sometimes, there is a lot of room.

2. Was it the best that could be done?

When I fall short of a goal, I don't blame the circumstances. As they say, when you miss the target, *it's never the target's fault.* Just because I didn't do it right, that doesn't mean someone with a different or higher-level skillset than mine couldn't have. For instance, if a presentation falls on its face, even if it was due to factors that were out of my control, I still think about what some of my colleagues would have done to overcome the setback and convert a dead event into a homerun. I know that somebody could have done it. The answer is out there, and I challenge myself to find it.

3. What was the difference?

When I evaluate myself, I ask, "What do they have that I don't?" thinking about my colleagues who, in my opinion, are better than I am. When I train at my workout class, I compare my form and skill to my instructor's. In business, I assess my leadership in relation to those I admire. I do this in every aspect of my life. This provides me an assessment of where I am and, more importantly, the skills I need to add in order to grow.

For instance, Kirk Nugent's poetry has a mesmerizing effect on audiences. He is a lyrical assassin on the microphone. There have been multi-speaker events in which the presenters before him did horribly, but he had the crowd in the palm of his hands. The way he flows is masterful. His style engages the right-brained thinking, creative people in the audience because of the rhythmic delivery of his lines. Because of this, he could go places I couldn't. I was inspired to figure out how to incorporate some of this magic into what I do.

After months of analysis, trial, and many errors, I figured it out. My objective was to create a series of "right-brained" moments that would have a similar effect as Kirk's poetry. I did this by mastering a handful of improv comedy games that I use to illustrate my points instead of a traditional lecture style.

Also, I added some additional tools by using props

that bring new life to that segment of the presentation. Now, although our styles remain very different, I can still hold my own.

You should be doing this exercise for every area of your life that you want to improve. Compare and contrast your results with the results of people you feel are ahead of you in the game. These people can be your contemporaries or your heroes. They don't have to be from this era. They don't even have to be living. Your objective is to dissect their work, study the intricacies of how they think, and learn the inside details about how they do what they do.

4. What will I do differently next time (in my performance and my preparation) to close the gap?

The rest is simple. Make a list of the skills you need to acquire and systematically implement them into your routine. Remember, anything worth being good at is worth being bad at until you get good.

Look in, Then Look Out

As you sit down and plan the next big move in your life, consider trying something different this time. Instead of making a list of what want to achieve, put the pen down, be still, and ask what your assignment is. When you get the answer, pursue it with everything you have. You will never regret that decision.

Your best days are ahead of you.

MAKE IT HAPPEN!

1. What is your temperament? Number each temperament from one to four. Write a "1" next to your primary temperament, "2" next to your secondary temperament, and so forth until you have ranked all of them. If you believe there is a tie between two temperaments, rank yourself according to which comes most naturally to you or the one in which you operate most frequently.

> ___ Director   ___ Energizer
> ___ Stabilizer   ___ Connector

2. What does this say to you about the jobs and assignments that suit you best?

_____

_____

_____

3. Keep the four performance review questions we just discussed in a file on your phone or computer. Use them as a template to evaluate your performance for five days. Look for trends, and most importantly, the habits you can fix to improve your performance.

PERSONAL NOTES

_____

_____

_____

_____

_____

IDEAS AND ACTION ITEMS

_____

_____

_____

_____

_____

_____

_____

_____

_____

_____

_____

IDEAS AND ACTION ITEMS

_____

_____

_____

_____

_____

_____

_____

_____

_____

_____

_____

_____

Get Off Your 'BUT' And
OVERCOME YOUR OBSTACLES

"When you are at a crossroads and it's all or nothing, choose all."

-Jonathan Sprinkles

I tried not to stare at him. It would have totally killed the moment. But I couldn't believe what I had just heard. Without my realizing it, my feet had completely stopped. I was temporarily frozen in my tracks. I'm talking about a scene backstage at a well-known event, but I'm getting ahead of the story.

I was in a small entourage, flanked by security, event reps, and a few family members. The "star" of the group was a very well-known Hollywood celebrity. He was enjoying the fruits of a burgeoning acting career, thriving business ventures, and being interviewed by every major television outlet under the sun. At the time, he was the "it guy" in America.

I looked upon him with supreme admiration because of the empire he and his team had built, so I was stunned when I heard what he mumbled under his breath. He sighed deeply, shook his head, and in exasperation, he uttered, "I wish...just for 15 minutes, I didn't have to be me. I wish every minute of my day wasn't obligated to someone else. I wish I could just relax without people pulling on me for one thing or another."

He wasn't being ungrateful. He was tired.

Never once had it occurred to me that, amidst all the success he was experiencing, there could possibly be an underside that was as unappealing as having millions of dollars in the bank and the world at your beck-and-call was alluring. In my naïveté, I completely overlooked the inevitable wear-and-tear that being one of the hottest names in Hollywood would bring about. In that brief, candid moment that I probably wasn't supposed to hear, I got the lesson of a lifetime: everything has a price.

Little did I know, that experience could not have come at a more perfect time for me. Shortly after the backstage event, my life and career took off. I was on television and in magazines what seemed like every other week. I was so consumed with interviews and writing articles, I had to put the normal affairs of my life on hold. If I wasn't speaking, I was studying or writing. It was my turn to have the "moment" that made me wish I could press pause on life and take a quick breather.

But that isn't the juicy part of the story. What you really want to know is what was happening behind the scenes while all this was going on. I was a wreck. I wasn't sleeping, eating, or exercising regularly. I had no focus, was alienating myself from the people closest to me, had turned into a quasi-recluse, and frequently battled feelings of overwhelm. The one phrase I kept repeating to myself was "keep moving forward." This was a reminder never to stop and think about how I was feeling because I already knew I'd fall into a slump. I didn't have the luxury of saying, "Why me?" because the answer would have set me on a path of self-pity and doubt about my future (mind you, this was taking place while I was in the midst of my career heating up).

As I have continued along my path, these and many more character-building moments have shaped my perspective on learning to prosper under pressure. One thing is very clear: life is always a mixed bag of bitter and sweet experiences. Even times of extreme success may be tempered by nagging thoughts of challenging circumstances lingering in the back of my mind. I have cashed big checks but had no peace at night. I have sat inside my "dream home" but felt lonely because a close relationship had recently gone awry. I have received great news but had nobody to share it with who could understand. At times, my company looked great to outsiders, but was chaotic internally.

> **At no point, however, should you allow your flaws and problems to hinder you from pressing toward the mark.**

It happens. Actually, I was comforted to discover that this paradox is common among many successful people. They learn to master the art of applying the Pareto Law in their favor. It states that 20 percent of your efforts will yield 80 percent of the results. This explains how someone can be brilliant in his or her field of business, inept in other areas, and still come out on top. I know doctors who, themselves, can't give up smoking. I know preachers who struggle with their faith. I know personal trainers who don't have an ounce of self-esteem. I know life coaches who have muddled personal lives.

Being successful doesn't equate to having it all together. Sometimes, "making it" means being willing to be a "public success and a private mess" until you get it together. **At no point, however, should you allow your flaws and problems to hinder you from pressing toward the mark.**

The hardcore reality is, you will never arrive at a place in your life where everything is running smoothly at the same time. Don't expect your setbacks to be polite and enter your life one at a time in a single-file line. They normally travel in packs, barging in unconcerned about whether or not they are interrupting a great moment. I used to believe the adage that problems come in three's. I wish! That's just the beginning. The initial three problems usually each get pregnant and give birth to twins!

> **When you buy into someone's point of view, you buy into the lifestyle that belief system creates.**

The bright side for you is that, when they do invade your life, there is a litmus test that will indicate if they will exist in your life long enough to reproduce another generation.

1. What you say to yourself.

What self-talk (internal dialogue) goes through your mind when you're under pressure? Do you spend more time thinking about what's happening to you or what you intend to do about it?

2. What you see happening.

Do you give yourself space to step back and look for patterns or habits that contributed to the event? Do you view it as character building or just bad karma?

3. Who you surround yourself with.

This is crucial. Would you characterize your confidants as generally positive or negative? Do they help you see blind spots you might have missed? Can you go to them with questions and walk away with answers? Here's the crucial question: Do you respect them? If not, why would you solicit their opinion? **When you buy into someone's point of view, you buy into the lifestyle that belief system creates.**

4. What outcome you will settle for.

What attitude do you have about conflict and overcoming adversity? Are you solely focused on surviving the storm or do you insist on learning the lesson that the storm was meant to teach you? Are you content with "getting over it" or are you determined to get a little better each time?

Knowing that ups and downs will be a part of the makeup of your life forever, the objective evolves from eliminating problems (which isn't going to happen) to maintaining your poise throughout. I call it learning how to "Move Your 20." You make a list of the actions that comprise the 20 percent that yields 80 percent of the results and, no matter what, you do not fail to do them. There are some elements of your life that may get reprioritized when you're under pressure. Never these. If circumstances are such that something in the 80 percent has to be turned in late or gets put on the backburner, it will hurt; but so be it. Your "20" consists of the indispensible, non-negotiable, mission-critical aspects of your life that drive progress. In essence, if everything else fell by the wayside and you only did these things, you could still make it.

Moving Your 20 means that you will do these things irrespective of other life events. When someone in your company quits, when you get a bad report from your doctor, when you get a certified letter in the mail stating you are being sued, when your spouse tells you that you've changed and he or she isn't interested in the relationship anymore, when your bills are piling up faster than your income can handle them, when you are depressed, when people are depending on you for answers but you don't have a clue how to figure things out, keep Moving Your 20! Establish your 20 and dedicate times in your daily routine to ensure that you do them without fail.

Author Dan Kennedy disclosed in one of his books that he wrote a particular chapter the morning of his mother's funeral. Even the sadness of his mother's passing couldn't interrupt the daily ritual that built his empire. Motivational speaker Dr. Kenneth McFarland shared a story about how he valued his health so much he walked every morning, rain, sleet, or snow, even if he was ill. His motto was, "If I can find a reason to take a pause, I can find a reason to stop." I was an eyewitness the morning when popular minister Dr. Dana Carson, only minutes from being released from the hospital where he had been treated all night, was clearly depleted physically but delivered his message to a packed house as if he were in peak condition. Seeing this showed me that he truly lives his own message that "if going backward ever becomes an option, going forward isn't." When your 20 is an immutable part of your life, you guarantee good results. People change; the weather changes; but this cannot change.

They say the key to wealth is to create multiple streams of income. The key to Moving Your 20 is creating a constant stream of focus. While you attend to issues of life that periodically arise, you never lose sight of what's important. You will develop the ability to keep one eye on that which demands your attention and the other eye on that which advances your vision. In school, your 20 was your coursework. In business, your 20 is your set of core money-making tasks. As a parent, your 20 is quality time spent with your child. As I compose this book, my 20 is being at the computer researching, writing, (and rewriting). Your 20 is immutable. It doesn't change with the circumstances. Even when the season passes on the events that are currently stressing you out, the work you put in Moving Your 20 still stands.

Now it's your turn. It's time to define your 20. In the space below, write the 10 activities that drive your business, career, and life, along with *why* they are important (i.e. why this versus something else?):

Your 20

_____
_____
_____
_____
_____
_____
_____
_____
_____

Why?

_____
_____
_____
_____
_____
_____
_____
_____
_____

Once you have identified your 20, be prepared to take them for a test drive. You may feel the need to amend your list slightly. Once you have gained clarity about what they are, give yourself a double bonus by ranking them in order of importance. In doing so, you will create your customized "in case of emergency" plan that will instruct you where you need to be placing your energy if resources become limited.

"Don't let what you can't do get in the way of what you can do."

The essence of overcoming adversity and Moving Your 20 is just that—moving. When you have to sometimes play through pain—keep moving forward. When you feel like your life is a walking contradiction—keep moving forward. When you are uncertain which people in your life have betrayed you and who is loyal to you—keep moving forward. When you're lonely, depressed, or feel like nobody understands you, cry for a minute but—keep moving forward! When you come out of your situation, you are guaranteed to have unparalleled clarity about who and what is most important in your value system. You will be remade and your strength renewed. You won't like it while it happens, but you'll be glad you pushed through it.

Your life will get better when you get better at life. **Don't let what you can't do get in the way of what you can do.** Move Your 20 and get your breakthrough.

MAKE IT HAPPEN!

1. What one habit would you like to change about yourself, specifically, in how you respond to being under pressure or facing a big challenge?

_____

2. List specific words you can use or past victories you can reference to make your internal dialogue more empowering.

_____

_____

_____

3. For one week, write your daily to-do list on a "Make It Happen List." For your convenience, one is located at www.GetAndStayMotivated.com. Use this tool to increase your focus, boost your productivity, accelerate and track your results, and celebrate your success.

PERSONAL NOTES

_____

_____

_____

_____

_____

IDEAS AND ACTION ITEMS

IDEAS AND ACTION ITEMS

_____

_____

_____

_____

_____

_____

_____

_____

_____

_____

_____

IDEAS AND ACTION ITEMS

Get Off Your 'BUT' And **ENLARGE YOUR VISION**

"Doubters see things as they are.
Believers see things as they can be."

-Jonathan Sprinkles

At the turn of every year, I am a busy guy. I am frequently requested by television, radio, and print media outlets to give my commentary on how to "make this year your year." Producers count on me to give their audiences a shot of hope accompanied by a dose of motivation. I don't let them down. However, I also throw another element into the mix: hardcore truth.

Hardcore Truth #1: "New year, new you" is a bunch of crap.

Nothing about your physical, mental, emotional, or spiritual makeup changes between December and January. Whatever challenges and opportunities you went to bed with on December 31st are going to wake up with you on January 1st. Your credit score doesn't improve; your bank account doesn't get a boost; and whatever weight you needed to lose, yup, it's still there... jiggling.

> The concept of having a time of year dictate when you are going to apply yourself toward your goals is just as dangerous as it is ludicrous.

The term "new year, new you" is cute, but highly inaccurate. The calendar was invented thousands of years ago for two main purposes: farming and rituals. They didn't create the 12 months of the year so you would know when to "name and claim" your Mercedes Benz or dream job! You've got to be kidding me. **The concept of having a time of year dictate when you are going to apply yourself toward your goals is just as dangerous as it is ludicrous.** January has no more power than April does. But we don't talk about our goals much in April because, statistically speaking, 87 percent of us have long abandoned them by then!

Does this bother you at all? Aren't you tired of doing the same thing and getting the same result? If so, read on. I have something for you.

Hardcore Truth #2: Your new diets, budgets, and resolutions are going to fail.

People, who are supposedly desperate to finally see change, ask me for help all the time.

"Jonathan, I've tried a million things," a lady recently told me.

I smiled, stared at her directly in the eyes, and responded, "No you haven't. You've repeated the same two or three things so frequently it feels like a million times. You've used the same strategy to achieve the same goal. The names of the programs you've tried have changed, but they're still missing a key ingredient and that is causing you to get inconsistent results."

I proceeded to explain to her that there are two different modes of operation: tactical and strategic. Tactics are your day-to-day behaviors. Strategy is the Ultimate Outcome that the behaviors are intended to create. Most "change programs" (diets, budgets, goals, etc.) emphasize the tactics; and because that is what you think will get you to where you want to be, you buy them. However, this is also the hidden reason why many of them don't create lasting results. The very name "diet," "budget," or "resolution" implies short-term behavior versus a lifestyle change. This explains why only 13 percent of us get beyond the first few weeks of the program before abandoning it.

Hardcore Truth #3: Change is a four-part formula.

Here's what most people *won't* **tell you. Your strategy should have four parts, not one: a vision, plans, goals, and action items.**

VISION

Lasting change requires long-term purpose. The way to get your goals to stick is to see yourself as you will be when you have achieved them. Performance psychologists conducted a study on a basketball team. For one week, half the team practiced as normal while the other half only visualized themselves practicing. They were taught how to create vivid images in their minds of flawless execution of their passing, dribbling, shooting, and defending. The half that only visualized their practice outperformed those who worked out every day.

> **You will always achieve the picture that you see most clearly in your mind.**

Your vision is the bridge between your present condition and your Ultimate Outcome. **You will always achieve the picture that you see most clearly in your mind.** For decades, gurus have espoused the value of A) clarifying your vision into one sentence and B) stimulating your mind by placing subconscious triggers around the areas you frequent most. Personally, I recommend you spend an evening creating a vision board if you don't have one yet. Cut pictures that represent your Ultimate Outcome out of magazines or download them from the Internet; then affix them to your wall or a corkboard, along with statements that affirm your vision.

QUICK WARNING:

1. Write the affirmation in affirmative language! "I'm not going to ABC anymore" or "I'm going to stop XYZ" isn't affirmative. State what you *are*, not what you are not.

2. Plan for the aftermath. Most performance coaches do a great job of encouraging you to make it to your goal. Awesome. But what happens once you reach it? I'll tell you what happens; you fall off!

The objective is to hit the number, but rarely is there mention of what happens afterward. It's like designing an awesome wedding but having no plans for the actual marriage. The assumption is that once you make it "there," you'll be motivated to stay there. But you know from experience this isn't true.

PLANS

Once you clarify the Ultimate Outcome, the obvious question becomes, *how am I going to do it?* Your plans are the glue that holds your vision together. Unfortunately, this is where most of us unknowingly fall short. We all know how to state what we want and even how we intend to make it happen. But there is something we often forget to factor in—the birds.

> **Birds come to us through various life events with the intention of distracting, detouring, delaying, or discouraging us.**

There is an ancient parable about a man who was sowing seeds in his field. The seeds fell on four different qualities of soil that allowed the seeds to either take root and grow or instantly die because the ground was unsuitable. Stony ground was the worst because the seeds could not penetrate it. They stayed at the top of the soil and ultimately became bird food.

Despite your grandiose dreams and carefully-laid plans, the birds are coming after the seeds of your dreams. They are going to make an attempt to eat up what you have laid out. **Birds come to us through various life events with the intention of distracting, detouring, delaying, or discouraging us.** Have you ever noticed that every time you set your mind to do something you need to do but have been putting off, an interruption always seems to pop up? This is not coincidence…it's the birds! As soon as you intend to sit down and study, someone calls with an "emergency" that has to be discussed immediately. As soon as you declare you are going to get serious about building your spiritual relationship, something in your life goes haywire. It happens every time. It's the birds!

Your plans have to account for the birds as much as they do the good times. These questions will provide a great start:

1. Who is holding you accountable other than yourself?

_____

_____

2. If you have to skip a day, what is your policy for getting back on track?

_____

_____

3. If a choice has to be made, what (or who) are you willing to give up in order to stay on your plan?

_____

_____

GOALS

Goals are, by far, the best-known part of the formula. They are also the most misused. We are taught how to "set goals," but few of us have ever been shown how to create self-perpetuating ones.

For starters, let's examine how many of us are setting ourselves up for failure from the beginning. We only talk about the goal, itself, ignoring how it fits into the plans or the vision. All we care about is the destination; such as the day we finally see "the number" on the scale.

Goals without deadlines are just requests.

This has happened to me, too. Some time ago, I was at an expo and walked by the booth of a gentleman who was conducting free health screenings. He took all my measurements and vital signs. Low and behold, I was 17 pounds overweight! I knew my pants were fitting a little snug around my thighs, but I thought it just accentuated the junk in my trunk. Little did I know, my trunk was packed with chunks of cellulite! I was floored. Until that point, I had never weighed that much above my target weight. My body mass index was off the charts, too. I was a hot, tubby mess.

I panicked. Knowing what I do about goal setting, I wrote, in big letters on the dry erase board in my office, *I weigh XXX pounds* [my ideal weight is withheld to protect me from your getting in my business if you see me looking out of shape some day]. I looked at the number all day, every day while I was working. While I was correct to put a number on my goal, the place where I screwed up was in omitting the part that motivates action—the deadline.

Goals without deadlines are just requests. For you to say, "I am a millionaire" or "I have a 3.95 grade point average" is a bold, aggressive move. Declaring it is a good place to start, but a terrible place to finish. The question you have to also answer is *by when?* It is the deadline that gives you the sense of urgency that compels you to get off your "but." If you only state the What but never the When, you have placed yourself on an indefinite timeline. It doesn't matter if you work toward it today, tomorrow, or next year because there is no due date. This usually translates to the goal being put on the backburner and reprioritized to accommodate other life events that come up. This is classic bird feed.

My friend and colleague James Malinchak, who was featured on a hit reality show called "The Secret Millionaire," built a public speaking business from literally a few sketches on scrap paper into a multi-million dollar empire. He is now one of the highest-earning speakers in the world. I have had the privilege of observing his ascent firsthand. (How cool is it to be able to say, "I watched someone become a millionaire.") After studying his ways on and off the stage, I have identified the one habit that has been most responsible for putting money in the bank—speed.

James doesn't mess around. He places a premium on completion. His now-famous motto, GSDF, stands for "Get Stuff Done FAST!" Getting stuff done is good; getting stuff done fast makes you rich. James is proof of what happens when you have a mindset that combines high goals that stretch you with the discipline to knock them out quickly. Speed is your secret weapon to big results.

Don't let your goals linger. Push yourself to shorten your deadlines so you can achieve quick outcomes, which will build your confidence. Success breeds more success. Don't just get stuff done…get stuff done FAST!

ACTION ITEMS

Believe it or not, this is the area most of us screw up more royally than the other three. This is because we are taught to write our daily action items like we do a grocery list. Before we go to the supermarket, we don't spend much time thinking about the most efficient manner to traverse the aisles from entry until checkout. Actually, I should say normal people don't do that. If you do, you are officially weird. I digress. When we make our grocery list, it is usually done in our kitchen as we take an inventory of the items we need to pick up at the store. Of course, this gives no regard to the relationship between the items other than that they will both end up in the same basket.

For your trip to Food R Us, this kind of list is great. For your day-to-day routine, it stinks. I have experienced on several occasions that nagging feeling when I realize I could have saved an hour by completing three tasks sequentially that were all related instead of crisscrossing my path. What's more, I have made myself shoutin' mad when I worked my butt off to nearly complete my list only to discover that the three most important items were at the bottom!

Before you start celebrating the death of all to-do lists, slow down. You may want to know this first: most successful and wealthy top achievers live by a list. Personally, I don't know one person making over $250,000 who doesn't rely heavily on one. Wherever you want to be, your list is your ticket out. Whatever you want to have, your list is your key to getting it.

For example, do you feel your chances of success would dramatically increase if you made a list like the ones described below?

- Your concerns before speaking with your spouse or significant other.
- Your top accomplishments before your next interview or performance review.
- People you want to meet who can be significant to your future.
- The skills you need to acquire in order to advance your career.
- The five milestones you need to hit to get promoted.
- Each exercise you do and the amount of time it takes to complete it.
- What you know for sure and the abiding values that you use to make tough decisions.

Your performance would be off the charts, wouldn't

it? Don't you feel like you could virtually guarantee any level of success you wanted? If so, you're right. I believe in the principle so much, I stopped doing to-do lists and took it to another level by designing a "Make It Happen List." You can do whatever works for you, but you have to follow a couple of rules.

Be CLEAR about the big stuff.

Not everything should qualify as an A-1, "must do right now" emergency. Actually, it is through those days that are so crazy that almost none of our list has been accomplished that we learn most of our list didn't have to get accomplished that day anyhow. While making it to the mall may take up the same amount of space on your to-do list, clearly it does not occupy the same level of importance as making it to the doctor. However, if your system is to simply check one item off and proceed down your list, you get yourself in trouble.

The trip to the mall throws off the rest of your schedule because you get caught up looking at something, lose track of time, and now you've missed your doctor's appointment. Trust me, the variables in this scenario may be different in your life, but this happens all the time. "B" priorities end up taking time away from the "A" priorities, and you find yourself feeling tired and unaccomplished at the end of the day.

Can I get an amen?

Here's the solution: prioritize. Discriminate even. Your task list should be written twice. First, get everything out on paper, then select the three High Value Tasks that you will build your day around. Meaning, if your day became so crazy, you only got to accomplish three things, what would they be? Essentially, what is your 20 for today?

This is difficult at first because we are so accustomed to valuing everything equally. Change that. Develop the skill of knowing when to say yes and when to say no, even when it hurts. High achievers rely on their ability to discriminate between what would be nice to do and what must be done.

Writing the vision of your day makes an appointment with your future. Get clear about what you want from it when it arrives.

Be CREATIVE about the rest.

After you have ordained your High Value Tasks— Your 20—managing the rest becomes a work of art. Start off by grouping similar tasks together. You can arrange them by time of day (morning, on the way home from work, etc.), location ("while I'm on that side of town"), or similar function (emails, phone calls, bills to be paid). This alone will multiply your efficiency by causing you to map out in your mind how you will go about conquering your list.

One hidden advantage to list making that is not exclusive to to-do lists but includes lists of all varieties is the way it ignites your creativity. Actually getting it down on paper so you can see everything in front of you is like putting all the puzzle pieces down at one time so they assemble to form the picture. Financial advisors recommend listing your monthly expenses so you can see for yourself what you have to work with. Self-help expert Jim Rohn teaches an exercise that brings people face-to-face with their future by instructing them to list 50 events they want to achieve over the next 20 years. Nothing is more exciting than seeing your best-case scenario laid out before your eyes. Once your heart's desires are written, you begin to attract into your life events that make them come to pass. Most importantly, your heightened sensitivity triggers you to take action as these opportunities arise. It's amazing. *You should do this. It really works!*

You are your habits.

You have to get your ideas out of your head and onto a piece of paper. I always preach, "in your head, ideas are dead; but what you write becomes real." Writing forces you to think through your ambitions and concretize what you really want. It also affords you the advantage of seeing everything in one place. Thus, you can get a snapshot of your plans in totality. At that point, you can judge whether you are satisfied with your ambitions or if you need to further challenge yourself to expand your vision. Finally, you ask yourself the million-dollar question: what do I have to do to make this happen? This is where your imagination kicks in, your strategic thinking takes over, and your blueprint for building your empire takes form.

Always be CONSISTENT.

Your new relationship, new car, or new six-pack abs don't hinge upon how badly you want the outcome. Oh no, no, no. It is determined by your daily rituals that create the outcome. Wanting it won't get you there. Working toward it consistently will. My mother has told me since I was a teenager, "What you do most is what you do best. Practice makes perfect, so be careful what you practice." **You are your habits.** If you want six-pack abs, you need some six-pack habits. If you want to be a millionaire, you need to start some million-dollar habits. Above everything else, focus on integrating into your routine the practices that will move you toward where you want to be. What you do today is a preview of what tomorrow will look like.

> **All you have to do is choose to be consistant.**

Your new routine will suck at first. Do it anyway. You don't have to like it. At first, you probably won't. But you will like the positive results and compliments it brings. You don't even have to be good at it. You do have to be consistent. You do have to keep showing up each day. You do have to overcome the temptation to back away, think small, or make excuses. You do have to understand that, just like everything else you've done, in time this will become second nature to you. You don't have to be the smartest person in your circle, the best looking, or have the best education or family background. You don't have to have the most money in your bank account. You don't even have to be the most skilled. **All you have to do is choose to be the most consistent.** My colleague Superwoman Entrepreneur Vicki Irvin teaches how this principle has made her and her husband, Lloyd, super rich. As she simply puts it, "The most consistent person always wins."

CELEBRATE your progress!

As a classic Type A person, I love a challenge. I thrive off of it. I live for the rush of overcoming obstacles then standing at the mountaintop, beating my chest in victory. Hey, it's a little dramatic, but it's my dream not yours. I love the feeling I get when I look at a job well done and finally get to say the line I use to give myself a pat on the back, "Yeah boy, you did that!"

The problem is, being a classic Type A, I usually reward myself for completing one project by…starting another one! Although I know better—I am admitting this to you in hopes of recovering—I am addicted to making things happen and making progress. But omitting the celebration doesn't keep the fire burning; it burns me out. A much smarter way to operate would be to have a set of daily rewards that are earned (or lost) based on productivity.

When I say the term "reward," most of us are so cynical these days, it doesn't elicit any emotional response. It does nothing to you to envision yourself earning a prize or special treat. I'm not talking about a grab bag at a five-year-old's birthday party, so let's not go there. Your reward is whatever you want it to be. The easiest way to reward yourself is to take something you already do habitually and hold it as a ransom until you have completed the rest of your list. How much more motivated would you be if Facebook, text messaging, listening to the radio in your car, or watching your favorite TV show was provisional, not an entitlement?

You see my point.

Once again, your reward is only good if it *means something to you*. I'm not giving you permission to go broke buying yourself expensive gifts or get fat by gorging on sugary snacks. If you do that, don't say I told you to! The purpose of the celebration is to momentarily pause from the action, take a look at what you've done, get a mental picture, create a positive emotional anchor, and recognize your success. So put that gallon of ice cream away!

Note: My "Make It Happen" lists have radically improved my focus and efficiency. I get so much more done than I used to! I'd love to share them with you if you want similar results for yourself. You can get some online at www.GetAndStay-Motivated.com. Please tell me what you think!

Act as if you already have what you want and you are what you intend to be. Your mindset and your habits are connected. Where the head goes, the body follows. Celebrate in advance. Prepare for your promotion. Write your tithe check now. Write the huge check to charity now. Write yourself a check in the amount you desire to one day deposit into your savings or retirement account. Go to the car lot and test-drive your dream car. Call a realtor and schedule a tour of a home you would love to own, but is way outside your budget. Cut out pictures of clothes that would look terrible on you now, but will be fabulous when you get in shape. Put them on a vision board. Regularly visit stores you currently can't afford until the sales reps at the stores know you by name. Make an appointment with your future!

Refuse to be defined by your circumstances. Treat your outcome as though it were already a reality. Even if you can't afford it (yet), you can still use your power of creative visualization to hone your kinetic antenna to prepare yourself for the blessing when it happens. Dreaming is the first part of becoming. Act as if, and it will be.

PERSONAL NOTES

_____

_____

_____

_____

_____

IDEAS AND ACTION ITEMS

IDEAS AND ACTION ITEMS

_____

_____

_____

_____

_____

_____

_____

_____

_____

_____

_____

IDEAS AND ACTION ITEMS

Get Off Your 'BUT' And **BOOST YOUR CAREER**

"Be the one they can't afford to let go!"
-**Jonathan Sprinkles**

I'm fed up. I can't take it anymore. I'm sick and tired of all these folks blaming people for their living conditions. In my not-so-humble opinion, we are the generation that, more than any time in history, is the most forward-thinking and technologically advanced, with the most opportunities and fewest barriers to success. Yet we complain more than people of any previous era. Entitlement runs rampant throughout our society, permeating all cultures, age ranges, and even socio-economic levels. We demand the "basic necessities" of life: cable television, the latest model cell phone, new sneakers, and wireless Internet service. We just *expect* things to fall into our lap. We feel it is our right to have a job—a good job—and whatever lifestyle we choose, even if it is more than we can afford.

Today, the national unemployment rate is staggering. There are currently 14.5 million unemployed people in the United States. With 9.2 percent of the population out of work, nearly everyone knows someone who is or has been unemployed for an extended period of time.

Get Off Your 'But' And

As unfortunate as this reality is for so many individuals and families, when I hear stories about people who have been out of work for the last two years, I can't help my reaction. My right eyebrow rises halfway up my forehead. My upper lip bunches up like something smells foul in the room. I make the "this doesn't make any sense" face. Then, against my own will, I blurt out a terse phrase that sometimes comes off sounding very insensitive.

"What? Seriously? Are you kidding me?"

I mean no disrespect, but I watch the news or read the paper every day. I see people starting over, learning new skills, and beginning new careers. People are finding work every single day. When I hear about someone going years and years without finding a job, it puzzles me. Does this mean no cars needed to be cleaned, no dishes needed to be washed, no kids needed tutoring, no phones answered, closets organized, walls painted, or meals cooked?

C'mon!

My brother lives in the San Francisco Bay area. When the economy initially began to change, he told me numerous stories of former Chief Technology Officers and IT Directors who went from six-figure jobs to bagging groceries and driving cabs. At the time, I felt sorry for them; but years later, my opinion has changed sharply. Whereas I formerly would have said what a shame it is that they have to compromise their quality of life, after many years of hearing similar stories (and worse) my response is *good for them!*

Here's why.

A few years ago, I flew to New York on business. I was asked to speak to a small group of top leaders on how to connect with their team members. Upon arrival at LaGuardia Airport, I grabbed my bags and hopped in a cab, preparing for a long ride even though I would be traveling only a few miles. New York traffic is infamous. In order to pass the time, I struck up a conversation with the cab driver.

As an aside, this is one of the many things I love about international hubs like New York. You can't ever judge someone based on looks alone. Texas is also very diverse; but the only dominant cultures are black, white, and Latino. That's it. But New York has an infinite array of cultures and subcultures that form a beautiful mosaic of people, all blended together on a little island on the East Coast. I have met people who looked like they could be my neighbors in Houston; but when I engaged them in conversation, French, Russian, or Portuguese flowed from their mouths. The person next to you on the subway could be a trash collector or the Prince of Zamunda. You never know. It is the most amazing feeling.

With this in mind, I was anxious to discover the origin of my cab driver's unique accent.

I asked, "Pardon me, sir. I don't mean to be nosey but…you have a distinct way of speaking. If you don't mind my asking, where are you from?"

He peered into the rearview mirror, almost looking shocked that I asked such a question. Perhaps that I even cared.

He replied, "I'm from a country called Ghana. It's in West Africa."

I nodded in acknowledgement. I was torn between asking more questions, sitting in silence while gazing at the Manhattan skyline, or getting all in this man's business. I couldn't resist.

"Sir, I don't meant to be nosey but…what brought you to America from Ghana?"

He paused for a few seconds, possibly wondering why I was so inquisitive. Was I just a nice guy or an undercover government agent? Carefully, he disclosed, "Well, my family immigrated here not long ago. I'm working so I can pay for my wife to go to school. When she gets her degree, I'm going to school and my wife will work."

> **In America, it doesn't matter where you start; it only matters where you choose to finish.**

"Wow, sir. That truly is the American Dream," I told him. "What you're doing is the very reason this great country was founded. I'm very proud of you and your family."

That instant, I was grateful to be in the presence of such a proud, hardworking man. Although I have to admit, I was a little freaked out by the fact that he had recently arrived in the country and was already driving cabs. Putting that aside, I became increasingly curious about his situation. I had to know more.

"Sir, I don't mean to be nosey but…Africa is pretty far. What made you come all the way over here just to go to school?"

He gazed at me again in the rearview mirror. But this time, it was with another look. It was the kind of look that said, "You've obviously missed the entire point." He took a deep breath, like he was about to pass down age-old wisdom from the ancestors.

He said something that forever changed my life. "In my country, if you are born poor, you will die poor. But in America, anything is possible for anyone. That's why we came here, because there are no limitations. **In America, it doesn't matter where you start; it only matters where you choose to finish.**"

That shut me up. I had nothing of value to say for the remainder of the short duration of the ride. His words penetrated my core, causing me to reflect on years of excuses, self-limiting beliefs, and destructive thoughts. Like scenes from a movie playing before my eyes, I reflected upon choice after choice that I had made to finish in the same place I started. Although I was relatively successful, I had bought into the "box" I was in, one based on what people "like me" typically do. That day, it all changed. My cab driver had become my personal messenger, here to show me what the phrase "it's possible" really meant.

Since that day, I have had little patience for people who complain about inconveniences and readjustments in their lives. In many cases, our nightmare is someone else's dream come true. That said, the context behind the hardcore, somewhat controversial philosophy I espouse about commanding your career begins to make sense. I don't believe an employer owes you anything beyond your salary. Recognition, rewards, and all that fun stuff definitely help, but they are not entitlements that come the day you are assigned a badge number. In a crowded marketplace with stiffer competition than ever before, you will rarely get what you deserve; but you will get what you demand. This begins with the demands you place on yourself. You may have a job, but are you intentional about doing your part to keep it? Are you becoming so valuable to your organization that letting you go or losing you to a competitor would impact their bottom line? Are you just occupying a cubicle or is your desk a hub for productivity? At the end of the day, this is what decision makers are looking at when they determine who hangs on another year, who moves up, and who gets the boot. When they lay out all the names and look at the performance numbers associated with each one, it becomes clear who is determined to succeed and who is meandering by, along for the ride.

Here's the most interesting part—history has proven that people who place high demands on themselves will succeed in any economy, boom or bust. They demand high results, regardless of the obstacles in their way. Conversely, those who give themselves over to being hypnotized by external factors will always struggle. Those

Get Off Your 'But' And

who want to prosper and demand that they prosper are always looking for ways to prosper. Those who prefer to blame are always looking for a scapegoat.

> ### Those who want to succeed, will succeed. Those who want to fail, will fail.

Let's turn back the clock to a time when things were *really* tough. The Great Depression was a worldwide economic depression preceding World War II. It lasted from 1929 until approximately 1940 and was the worst financial landscape anyone had ever seen. To date, nothing has come close. Think about it; an entire decade of widespread financial destitution! Times weren't just bad; they were awful—for everyone. Yet, there were still a few brave individuals who, choosing not to be victims of their circumstances, made a few gutsy moves, and reaped immense fortunes as a result.

In Kentucky, a grandfather named Colonel Harland Sanders started selling fried chicken at his gas station. By 1937, he expanded to a 142-seat restaurant to fill the growing demand. Around the same time, two young electrical engineers Bill Hewlett and Dave Packard became business partners and started their business in a rented garage. Commercial titans John Deere, Reynolds Aluminum, and Douglas Aircraft were also founded during that period.

The message is clear: **Those who want to succeed, will succeed. Those who want to fail, will fail.** The economic, political, and social climates are inferior barriers to those with self-determination. For those without it, these obstacles are the perfect excuse for their inability to overcome the odds. Don't get me wrong. I live in the same world you do. I know how difficult it is when life takes you out at the knees. I'm sure that nobody wants to fail. Nobody wakes up in the morning and says, "I really hope I get some bad news and my life takes a nosedive today." But let's face it; few of us are doing much to prevent ourselves from failing, either. Competition has increased across the board, even for entry-level positions. People who used to make hiring and firing decisions are now looking for jobs themselves. Unless you are aggressively adding more knowledge, more skills, and thus, increasing the value of your position, you are setting yourself up to be on the losing side of the

You can enjoy prosperity in any economy, but first you have to make yourself relevant!

statistics. You will be one of the 14.5 million people who were squeezed out of the job market because they failed to become indispensible to their employer or attractive to another company in their industry.

It isn't personal; it's business. This is what makes me blow my top when I read and watch stories on the news about people misleading the American public by blaming everything else but ourselves for our lethargic attitude about our work ethic and our careers. Colonel Sanders made tens of millions of dollars—beginning at age 65—while most people in the country were forced to ration their resources. Doesn't this say something to you? At every point in history, people will always buy what they want, whether they can afford it or not. This holds true for food, products, services, and for *you!* **You can enjoy prosperity in any economy, but first you have to make yourself relevant!** Become the luxury item your company will splurge to have. Stop asking the government to provide more jobs and start asking yourself how you can acquire a more valuable skillset. This is the only assurance you will ever have in life about maintaining your economic status.

I am always shocked when I hear people say, "I got laid off. I don't know what I'm going to do now." For real? You mean, you never thought about what you would do if you weren't in your current position? You thought everything was always going to be the same…forever? You had to know that your career was going to end one of three ways—you would work there until you retire (which was highly unlikely), you would decide to move on to another company, or they would put you out. These days, the latter option is the most common, so it is crazy to live without a contingency plan.

Now more than ever, the only thing constant is change. Organizations are being challenged to make tough decisions about how to slim down their expenses in order to remain competitive or stay in business. No position is perpetually safe. Even tenure doesn't mean what it used to anymore. Therefore, you need to get out of denial and prepare yourself for any turn of events. You should always be thinking about what you would do if you were called into the office and told your services weren't necessary anymore (also known as, *you're fired*). After you clean out your desk, then what? The event may be a disappointment, but it should never be a total surprise.

This is the principle behind why the government mandates that if you own a vehicle, you have to maintain insurance on it. Although we all hope not to have an unfortunate experience on the road, we must be prepared just in case we do. The same is true for your career—if you stay ready, you don't have to get ready. I have outlined some career-boosting strategies that will not only cause you to think through what would happen if your job were in jeopardy, but also help you avoid the scenario entirely. These tactics are your key to adding value to your organization and enhancing your personal brand.

1. Get Fired!

Fire yourself. Ask yourself, "If I had to reapply for my position tomorrow, why would they hire me over someone else?"

- When you are sick or on vacation, how much work goes undone until you return?
- How many people around you have a more versatile skillset?
- Do you have any specialized knowledge or expertise that requires people to rely on you to complete the team's projects?
- When people have questions or need insight, do they consult you first?
- If I interviewed your co-workers would they all say, without question, you are the strongest member of your team?

Take a long, honest look at how you stack up compared to your peers. Use this inventory as motivation to shore up your weaknesses and to reposition yourself according to your competitive advantages. How many superlatives can you use when describing yourself (e.g. first, only, fastest, most)? What aspect of your performance is unique to your organization? This is where the money is. Your reasons for getting rehired will be their reasons for keeping you on or promoting you when it's time.

2. Change Your Identity

Investigate other job functions within your organization. Don't be satisfied with only knowing your own role. You need to demonstrate that you could fill a spot in another department if your position were unexpectedly cut. "One" is the worst number in the new economy. Being versatile keeps you from being pigeonholed and prevents you from being stuck in a position longer than you care to stay there. Being able to solve multiple problems across several platforms makes you a value-added hire.

If your organization pays for continuing education classes, certifications, or immersion experiences, take them! All of them. These are free career boosters. They're essentially *paying for you* to make more money because your knowledge base will cause you to be worth more to the company. Being a lifelong learner as a principle is so important that even if they didn't reimburse you, the classes are still worth the investment. Take as many courses and get as many letters behind your name as necessary until you have advanced-level mastery of your topic of interest. Become the shizzle at what you do! An above-average skillset multiplies your value exponentially. You become a rock star at work and it makes you attractive to other potential opportunities within your marketplace. Jim Rohn always taught, "Your formal education will make you a living. Your self-education will make you a fortune." You can't always guarantee you will be the most intelligent among your peers, but you can always make yourself the most educated.

3. Send Your Boss Packing

When it is promotion time, the people who leapfrog their competition are the ones who have already proven that they have the skills for the job. A great "power move" that says "I'm ready for the next level" is to take some of your supervisor's work off of his or her plate so they can focus on other tasks. Offer to coordinate the staff meetings or assist with analyzing data.

There is a part of every job that your higher-ups hate doing. Ask, "If there were two things that would make your life easier if you could get rid of them, what would they be?" Use this to get your foot in the door. Faithfully perform these tasks on a high level like you were trying to prove a point—because you are. You show them that you can handle your job responsibilities and are ready for a preview of the next level of action. You will get invaluable experience and your supervisor will thank you for the relief.

4. Watch Your Mouth

People talk. And yes, people talk...about you! You can't control what they're saying, but you can control whether or not it is true. Don't allow yourself to get caught up in conversations about what's wrong with your company. In times of change and uncertainty, the negative folks come out of the woodwork. They love

> **What matters is who knows you and has the power to get you where you want to be!**

to start side conversations outside of meetings, trying to recruit people to their pessimistic point of view. Beware... these are the first people to get cut.

Develop a reputation for being the most positive and optimistic person in the office. Start with smiling more often in the hallways. Be the one person who says, "Good morning" to everyone when you walk in the door. You may think this is pointless, but people remember things like this. Some people rely on others' small acts of kindness such as these to get their day started right. One deed of overt enthusiasm can have a perpetual effect on your entire team.

In meetings, even if all you can say is "We're all in this together and we will figure it out," that still goes a long way for the morale of the organization. Nobody ever complains about someone being too encouraging.

Build Your List

Do you remember that before contacts were stored in our phones, we kept "little black books" of important people we knew? They were pointless. This totally misses the point of building a powerful personal brand. It doesn't matter who you know. In many cases, it doesn't even matter who knows you. **What matters is who knows you and**

has the power to get you where you want to be! You can know 1,000 people and be known by another 10,000; but if these people aren't responsible for making the decisions, outside of making you very popular, what does this do for your goals? Other than getting a lot of comments on your Facebook fan page, what have you accomplished?

The only list that matters is the one that has results tied to it.

- How many decision makers know what you do?
- How many of them are aware of your goals?
- How many of them have you served in order to stay on their radar, foster goodwill, and build the relationship?

Don't just strive to be well known. Become known by the *right* people. Meet the people who can give you insider information about upcoming changes, who can teach you who to be wary of, or who have the power to keep you off the chopping block when layoffs happen. Having friends in "high places" guarantees that you never end up on the wrong side of surprises. Who are the top three-to-five key players in your organization? In your industry? According to Hall of Fame speaker and "Referral Coach" Bill Cates, these are the people with whom you must immediately begin building relationships because of the magnitude of their network. Knowing these folks can make the difference in your career and your life.

An ancient proverb teaches, "Walk among the wise and become wise." Networking wizard Bob Burg shares practical advice on how this is done. "Position yourself as a Center of Influence—the one who knows the movers and shakers. People will respond to that, and you'll soon become what you project."

True! A quick way to elevate your status with insiders is to be affiliated with other insiders. You have to manage the perception game. The assumption is that if you are attached to so-and-so, you must have their stamp of approval and are a part of the crew. And then, people treat you accordingly.

You may not like what I'm about to say, but it's important you hear this. This world is run by alliances. In some circles, they are referred to as "strategic partnerships." The vast majority of deals that impact you and me occur within a tight-knit inner circle. People select from among their own and do favors for their friends. For everyone on the outside—too bad.

> **It isn't on them to tell you how you're doing. It is on you to ask!**

Some people know this as "getting the hook-up." Having a relationship with the right people can open doors that will change your life. But this comes with a strong warning—you have to be "hook-upable!"! This means it is in your best interest to be qualified, prepared, and darn good at what you do. In order to gain the attention of people in power and the respect of your peers, you want to demonstrate more than having potential; you must have a proven track record. You have to be a "sure thing" so the person giving you the hook-up isn't taking a risk; they are accelerating what was eventually going to happen anyhow.

A secret phobia shared by Centers of Influence is being embarrassed by the person to whom they gave their stamp of approval. If you were to mess up, their name would be connected to your gaffe. It goes down as a sign of their bad judgment. I know from experience what an awful feeling it is to have people look at me crazy when someone I recommended makes a you-know-what of themselves. It cuts like a knife when they say, "Hey, isn't that your boy who just screwed up?" Ouch! Trust me, Centers of Influence are always looking for people to promote and connect with other influential people, but not at the expense of the reputation they've meticulously worked to build.

Sure, some under-qualified people get the hook-up, but don't rely on it. We have all seen someone get access to or be locked out of something strictly because someone on the inside influenced the decision. The most talented singer doesn't always get the record deal. The best actor doesn't always get the part. The smartest person doesn't always get the award. The most qualified applicant doesn't always get the job. Fair or unfair; love it or loathe it; this is a fact of life. The hook-up sometimes trumps everything, but the one thing it cannot do is guarantee long-term success. That's your job. You should always focus on the quality of your work and the integrity of your reputation. Their word can get you in the door, but your work gets you respect.

Rather than fight the system, embrace it because it isn't going to change. Instead, use it to your advantage. Work super hard, get noticed, make the connections, and serve your way into the inner circle. As your "list" grows, so will your influence...and your income!

5. Pop the Question

Your performance review shouldn't be the only time you and your higher-ups talk about where you stand. Their final appraisal should not be a surprise. Take the guesswork out of it and create an ongoing dialogue about your contributions and the areas you need to develop. The foundation of every functional relationship is communication. When there is an open line of communication, you eliminate unexpected bombshells that erode trust within the relationship. If you two are constantly reviewing and refining your performance during the evaluation period, you should know before you go into the meeting what your scores will be.

Mind you, this dialogue is not the responsibility of your boss, who has other things to think about and, most likely, other people to lead. **It isn't on them to tell you how you're doing. It is on you to ask!** A savvy "career engineer" would set up this conversation as a periodic ritual to maintain top-of-mind awareness.

There are a couple of key action items that make this initiative a success. Communication specialist Pamela Jett (who has a featured interview in the *Get Off Your 'BUT' and Make it Happen Success Series* at www.GetAndStay-Motivated.com) teaches that you should create a Glory File that contains highlights and kudos. When your boss, peers, or customers send you a complimentary email, print it out and put it in your Glory File. When you have a noteworthy accomplishment or score a key victory, take the time to write a brief outline of the event, print it, and put it in your Glory File. There is nothing like having cold, hard facts when you need to state your case for promotion.

Career counselor Penelope Trunk recommends that you learn to "talk like your boss." Not everyone excels in face-to-face interactions. The last thing you want to do is make your supervisor uncomfortable. Forcing the issue could make your idea backfire in your face. Ask what method of communication he or she prefers: a daily list of accomplishments and questions, a weekly summary, or a short conversation. Trunk further cautions not to get caught up in so much detail that your report becomes cumbersome. Keep it simple. Bulleted, categorized lists will be received much better than paragraphs in small print.

Ask a ton of questions. Talk about the future of the organization and where you fit into it. Learn about the sources of stress and pressure your boss is facing. The more you two talk, the more productive you will become. You will transition from an employee to an ally.

6. If It Ain't Broke, Fix It Anyway

Most employees are paid between $10 to $50 an hour to work in the company's system. Most consultants are paid between $100 to $500 an hour to correct inefficiencies within the company's system. Which pay scale is most attractive to you? Just because you are a W-2 employee, that doesn't prevent you from having an entrepreneurial mindset. Think of yourself as a consultant who has been hired by your company to solve a problem in your department. You just happen to have a long-term contract.

One of my colleagues tells a story about how he used this technique to leverage a $50,000 raise. He didn't just go to work, do as he was told, and go home quietly. He saw that there were some gaping holes in his company's processes that were causing them to lose huge sums of money. He drafted a proposal to management, telling them that he would happily provide a solution that would save them hundreds of thousands of dollars annually. All they had to do was agree to raise his salary by $50,000 if his plan worked. He created such a compelling case, it was impossible to say no. Once his solution was in place and was proven successful, he doubled his salary!

Keep your eyes peeled for ways to improve the flow of work. Just because a workplace system is accepted by everyone doesn't mean that it's being done right. Most offices are steeped with inefficiencies, but nobody wants to do anything about it. We all have tasks that make us mumble, "This doesn't make any sense," but we do them anyway because we're too busy to figure out a better way. The stage is set! Be a consultant. Figure out a faster, more efficient, lower-cost way to get things done. You will become a hero in your office.

I do agree that times are tough, but not for everyone. For all the morbid talk about gloom and doom, you would think the world was coming to an end—tomorrow. Don't believe the hype! For every story on the news that projects all of the negative aspects of our society, there are plenty of stories (most of which will never make the headlines) that would give you hope and confidence about the future. And there are plenty. Some entrepreneur is enjoying record prosperity right now. Some couple is mending their differences and choosing to stay together right now.

Some patient is being released from the hospital, having won the battle over a major illness right now. Some first-generation college student is preparing to graduate with high honors right now. Someone has gone from unemployment or underemployment to getting their dream job—with a signing bonus—right now. You know why? Because they're placing demands on themselves to succeed and refusing to be denied. They're getting off their 'BUTS' and making it happen. If it can happen for them, it can happen in your household, too. Keep the faith. Put in the work. Things aren't bad for everyone. Most importantly, they don't have to be bad for YOU!

MAKE IT HAPPEN!

1. Start your Glory File.

2. Schedule a monthly performance review with your boss to learn how you can improve and become invaluable to your organization.

3. Write your "List" of decision makers that currently have your back. If you don't have anyone on your List, or are dissatisfied with it, make a separate list of the people you want to eventually have on your List.

PERSONAL NOTES

_____

_____

_____

_____

_____

_____

_____

_____

_____

_____

_____

IDEAS AND ACTION ITEMS

_____

_____

_____

_____

_____

_____

_____

_____

_____

_____

_____

_____

IDEAS AND ACTION ITEMS

Get Off Your 'BUT' And
BUILD POWERFUL RELATIONSHIPS

"All great relationships start with defining your commitment. Are you: Interested, Involved, Invested, or Committed?"

-Jonathan Sprinkles

BOLD CONFESSION: I am a recovering people pleaser.

I was just thinking this morning about how many times in my life I compromised myself in order to make other people happy. I was deathly afraid of conflict or being thought of negatively. The worst thing that could possibly happen to me was to know that you didn't like me. I would change whatever part of me you didn't like, whether it was authentic or not. It didn't matter as long as you were happy.

This mindset influenced every relationship I had— professional, romantic and platonic—dating back to my earliest memories in elementary school. Quite honestly, I don't know where it came from. Perhaps it was the byproduct of my quest for identity as the baby child of my blended family. Maybe it was an unexpected consequence of being forced to watch "One Life to Live" every single day of summer vacation when my sisters refused to change the channel. Maybe I was just soft.

I own my inner wimp. I'm actually very grateful for the man he made me become. I became so tired of "playing myself" over people who didn't really like me, I finally wised up, toughened up, and set some new "rules of engagement." I am now very clear about what works for me and what never will, no matter how hard I try. Some people are a good fit; some aren't. It doesn't make one of us bad and the other good; it's just a matter of congruence.

> **The degree to which each partner feels the other occupies a unique space in their life and provides an irreplaceable benefit is an indicator of whether or not the relationship will pass the test of time.**

My many mistakes have taught me to value synergy as the foundation of a successful partnership. The strength of the relationship hinges upon each party having clarity about who they are, what they bring to the table, and how they can use their abilities to fulfill their counterpart's needs. **The degree to which each partner feels the other occupies a unique space in their life and provides an irreplaceable benefit is an indicator of whether or not the relationship will pass the test of time.** Both sides have to believe A) this is a perfect fit for me and B) I can't find it anywhere else. This requirement sounds lofty, but it is also why so many relationships are failing these days.

If you're paying attention, you understand that I'm not referring to only one kind of relationship. Yes, I'm talking about business ventures, but I'm also talking about friendships. I'm talking about organizations. I'm talking about love. I'm talking about life.

Relationships of all varieties are pervasive throughout your life. This is why it is essential for you to grasp the concept I'm about to share. Your future will be heavily influenced by the quality of advice you receive from those who surround you. Mark Victor Hansen, co-creator of *Chicken Soup for the Soul*, asserts, "Your network determines your net worth." People hire, promote, and do business with people they like. Peter Drucker highlighted this fact when he stated, "More business decisions occur over lunch and dinner than at any other time, yet no MBA courses are given on the subject." Your success will be predicated not upon what you know, but by the question Keith Ferrazzi asks in the title of his bestselling book *Who's Got Your Back?* You won't just need relationships; you will need the *right* relationships to get you to the next level. Do the right people currently have your back?

Get Your House in Order

As a teenager, my mother would always admonish me, "Son, don't be inviting people over if your room isn't clean." I now realize that what she was teaching me wasn't just about vacuuming the floor and making my bed. She was giving me a life lesson about relationships. A muddled emotional life is akin to a messy home; inviting company adds more chaos to an already cluttered situation.

As you prepare yourself to add new relationships in your life, first straighten out areas of your life that you know need to be brought into order. This is the initial step of becoming relationship-ready. Reason being, any area in which you are still stuck in the past will become a potential weakness in your new relationship. If you still harbor any feelings at your former person, the new person will catch residuals. For instance, if you had an unpleasant experience with your supervisor at your last job, more than likely, you will be unnecessarily defensive at your next job. As an entrepreneur, I have gone through painstaking efforts not to let fear, anger, or resentment from being sold out by a former insider keep me from ever trusting anyone else with confidential information about my business. It happens to us all.

Let's keep it real; you could spend the rest of your life working on yourself before you became the perfect mentee, business partner, or spouse. No relationship will ever be perfect because no two people are perfect. But there are some rules for connecting with a Center of Influence. Until now, I have only shared these with clients, mentees, and those in my inner circle.

> **Becoming someone's mentee doesn't equate to your becoming their responsibility.**

RULE #1—THEY HAVE IT; YOU WANT IT.

They set the rules of the relationship and you follow them. It is what it is. Don't trick yourself into believing that you have a level of power or influence that justifies an attitude or your being anything but grateful. You have zeal and optimism, but they have something much more valuable—hindsight. You have exuberance; they have experience. I am constantly amazed by how many people I encounter who haven't grasped this. Your mentor doesn't owe you anything! If they missed your birthday or forgot that you had a big interview, get over it. If they don't call and check on you, then you call to give them updates. **Becoming someone's mentee doesn't equate to your becoming their responsibility.** They may be the top priority in your life; but with all due respect, you probably aren't theirs. If you thought highly enough of them to ask them to be your mentor, chances are you were not the first one to feel this way about them. More than likely, you were one of many. But all hope isn't lost. Being one of many still bears opportunity. You can elevate your status with them by positioning yourself to be the most enthusiastic, most thoughtful, most prepared, fastest-implementing, biggest-results-getting mentee they have. Even in a crowded space, you can separate yourself from the pack by choosing to go beyond what is expected of you.

RULE #2—DEFINE YOUR ROLES AND GOALS.

Inviting new people into your life is scary. Forrest Gump would say, "it's like a box of choc-lates because you never know what you're gonna get." Most people are great; but every now and then, there are a few characters that irritate the you-know-what out of you. There are the leeches who want to "pick your brain" all the time; the bug-a-boo's who call or email you several times daily; the chatterboxes who will keep rambling on the phone, even if you put the receiver in your desk during the middle of the conversation. And then there is the largest, deadliest group of them all—the time-wasters.

Time-wasters are a clandestine group. They don't have any traits that are identifiable to the naked eye. They're slicker than any *007* secret agent wishes he could be. They operate in stealth, appearing to be normal humans, until one day you look up and realize...yikes...you haven't accomplished anything since they arrived!

Time-wasters have been the undoing of many a great idea. Have you ever wondered why nobody has fixed the Liberty Bell and it still has that same crack in it hundreds of years later? Time-wasters. The Leaning Tower of Pisa is still tilted. You know some architect could have straightened it by now. Why not? Darn time-wasters.

People in authority try to avoid time-wasters like politicians avoid taking responsibility. They use secretaries, voicemails, or junk mail filters as their lines of defense

Get Off Your 'But' And

against them. If you want to get in with powerful people, you have to prove to them that you're not a time-waster in disguise. The fastest way to do this is to use this line:

If you are willing, I would like to learn (name of skill) from you. My promise to you is that I will follow your instructions to the letter and report back to you only when and how it is most convenient for you.

In the profound words of celebrity chef Emeril Lagasse, "BAM!" Successful people want to give back, but they don't want to be drained in the process. State your business, be clear about your purpose, and watch how their resistance melts away.

RULE #3—FIND YOUR FIT.

For all my talk about respecting the value of an adviser in your life, the flip side is that your best results will occur when you have a relationship with someone with whom you share a connection. Don't get me wrong; there are some people whose career or life you revere so highly, they could talk about your mother and it would still be cool. I get it. Those people, we can put into a special category. But for the majority of people who will be advising you, having a good vibe with them is everything.

I have created a short list of questions that will help you determine if your potential mentor/adviser is a good fit for your value system.

- **Do you admire them?**
  You will emulate what you envy most about people. If you deem them worthy of your admiration, you wouldn't mind becoming just like like them, or at least trading places. You won't

second-guess the soundness of their advice or feel the need to pick-and-choose which parts to follow.

- **Do they genuinely like you?**
  Do they have good feelings about you, show an interest in you, and look forward to talking to you? If you don't believe they do, you will wonder if you are bothering them and won't be assertive in your relationship with them. You will feel like an intruder rather than an insider. Conversely, when you two share an affinity, the relationship takes on a personality beyond its primary purpose. It is a joy, not a chore.

- **What is their reputation among their peers?**
  Politics are a part of every organization. If you align yourself with someone who is unpopular among the group, you, too, may be marginalized by the association. Be careful.

- **Are they good at teaching and explaining a process or are they a "just watch me" leader?**
  Some people are equippers; others rely on modeling. Depending on your learning style, one will produce significantly better results for you than the other. You want to align yourself with someone who knows how to say it so you get it.

- **Do you agree fundamentally with the guiding principles that they use to make decisions?**
  Their philosophy determines their morals, which determine their character. Learning their guiding principles will quickly let you know whether you identify with them or not.

- **Who are their heroes and why?**
  Knowing their heroes gives you a peek into where

they're headed in life and how they'll treat people along the way.

- **Would they feel comfortable if you had to open up to them about personal issues?**
  How "real" can you get with them? It doesn't mean they become your therapist. That is inappropriate. But can you go off-script or off-the-record with them? Can you confide in them and feel safe? This is the true measure of any relationship.

RULE #4—STAY COACHABLE.

The fastest way for you to flush a great relationship down the drain is to lose your humility. Remember that each of you has a role. Their job is to share their experiences and advise you accordingly. **Your job is to listen closely, absorb everything they tell you, write it down, and follow their advice.**

Success can be deceptive. The first thing people tend to do when they start to get their mojo working is to forget what got them there. It is like what happens when adolescents emerge into their own identity during the teen years. We all did it. Many of us fell out with our parents and even questioned their sanity at times. All of a sudden, we knew everything and our parents, who had fed, clothed, and nurtured us, were dumb as rocks. The day we could stand on our own two feet, we doubted whether the wisdom that got us there was valid anymore.

This analogy holds even truer when you consider where teens are in relation to the overall scope of their lives. They have a form of independence, but don't yet have a clue about how things work in a greater context. They think they do. They swear they do. But they don't.

It would have been foolish for you at 15 to argue when being advised by people who had walked your path and dealt many times with what you were facing. And guess what...it still is just as foolish for you to not remain coachable, regardless of how many years of experience you have under your belt.

One of my clients runs a high-six-figure martial arts training business. When he first applied to have me coach him, very honestly, I was puzzled. "He doesn't need me," I said (internally—I kept a straight face with him). He's already very wealthy. What in the world would someone who is making this kind of money want with me?" My own self-limiting thinking had taken over. Fortunately, he answered my questions before I had to ask. "Jonathan, let me tell you why I'm joining your program. You're teaching me something I can't find anywhere else. I can get mentored in other parts of my business in the $100,000 business building program I'm already enrolled in. But if I can get just one idea from you in your area of expertise, I've already earned my investment back. I can take the one idea and turn it into six-figures. I don't need much. Just give me one great idea and it's on."

Another client flies in from Canada once a year to meet with me. He creates wealth succession plans for high-net-worth families ($50 million and above). He's accustomed to being around big money. During our working lunch, the teacher became the student. He put his fork down, leaned toward me, almost looking troubled, and said, "Why don't you have a program that caters to high-level executives, Jonathan? You are a natural fit. Rather than working with 500 people, you could work with one person who influences 500 people." Wow. I hadn't even thought of it that way. Not once. Had I been caught up in my ego because of my position as his coach, I would not have listened and may have missed a $750,000 idea! Lesson: don't just check your ego at the door; bury it in your backyard. Choosing to value your image over sound wisdom can be the most expensive decision you'll ever make.

RULE #5—REPORT YOUR RESULTS.

Your progress reports are the coals that stoke the fire in the relationship and keep you on your mentor's radar. This is what keeps them interested in you. Personally, I love hearing updates from people I've touched throughout the years. Tess, who was in the audience when her college invited me to be a part of their distinguished lecture series, sent me a message on Facebook, which I saved. In the middle of her letter, she warmed my heart—

And I remembered that I live in a country where anything is possible. So now I have a 4.0 and just wanted you to know that it was because of what you said that day.

Brian checks in with me monthly to get pointers on how he can better run his organization. Chaunté and I do a victory dance every time she gets another promotion due to the leadership strategies I taught her. Kasey and I celebrate every time he steps out on faith and follows his true passion. Natalie has become unstoppable in her new career and follows closely in my footsteps by reaching back to develop those behind her. She introduces me to all of the new inductees in her team. The list goes on. I teach my people to always stay in the faces of Centers of Influence and let them see the fruits of their labor. It is an outstanding networking strategy…and it gets your name printed in books!

There are two very important times you will want to check in. The first is immediately following a call or meeting with them to confirm your action items and due dates. FYI—nobody does this! It is one of the most brilliant moves a mentee can make. Providing a short recap of the conversation and an action plan speaks volumes about you. It says you were listening, you were taking copious notes, and most importantly, you intend to take action. This is a defining moment. No mentor, coach, or adviser wants to waste their time. When you take this critical step, you position yourself in their mind as a good investment. Most people who have made it to the top did so by working extremely hard and going the extra mile. This move is sure to engender a stronger bond because you will remind them of themselves when they were at your level. This is a very good thing.

The second time to check in is when your action items have been completed. This is when the magic happens. Assuming you have handled your business, you should have a lot to report. Create a list of "you told me to do this, and these were the results" items. Discuss what you learned in the process. Ask follow-up questions. They will eat it up.

BONUS RULE—SAY THANK YOU. OFTEN.

One of my greatest joys in life is to help people get to (and through) college. One of my goals in life is to make it possible for every deserving student to have the opportunity to pursue higher education. That said, you can understand my sorrow when I met a young lady who had recently dropped out due to financial challenges. I called on a few people I knew in higher education, and they connected her to some people who could help her.

Months and months went by without any word about her progress. I didn't ask because I was busy and assumed her classes were going well. One day, I approached her and casually asked, "Hey, how's school coming?" She looked at me puzzled, as if to say, "You haven't heard?" I feared the worst.

"Um...I graduated. Last semester," she said.

My feelings of congratulations were quickly overshadowed by the realization that...*this girl finished school and didn't tell me!* I called the contacts who had helped her get back in school. They hadn't heard anything either. Not a word. This young lady had graduated college and hadn't sent even scribbled "thank you" on an old napkin!

> **The more frequently you praise your mentors for their efforts, the closer your relationship becomes.**

By far, that was the most egregious non-thanks I have ever seen, but there have been many others. Because of this, I am very clear and upfront that this is a "family value" I challenge my clients and mentees to adopt immediately. No matter what else they have going on at the time, "busy" is not an excuse. I tell them, "If you had time to pick up the phone and ask for help, you have time to send a thank you note for the help you received." You will look like a moron if you say you "haven't had a chance" to appreciate those who did things for you. People catch on quickly. Next time, they may not "have a chance" to answer the phone when you call.

As it pertains to building relationships, your expressions of gratitude are like mortar that keeps you and that person tightly connected. **The more frequently you praise your mentors for their efforts, the closer your relationship becomes.** Here's why—it helps you remain humble and it replenishes their reservoir of goodwill for you. Let's once again get in their head for a moment. Consider the psychological profile of many people in power. They are usually Type A personalities. They are very driven, don't have a lot of time for BS, and are always focused on results. Most importantly, they are being pulled on daily due to the nature of their position. With power comes responsibility...and stress. All day long, someone is asking them for something. When you show up in their day bearing something that gives them a reprieve from the rat race, you are an oasis in the desert.

My one big rule (and warning) is that digital thank you's don't count. Not with this group of people. Text messages and emails have become way overused. They are great for touching base, but they get read and deleted. They definitely don't touch the heart and create a lasting emotional connection, which is your goal. You can do better.

A good, heart-felt letter of appreciation has become more rare than a virgin on a reality TV show. This is your opportunity! Mix it up with cards, letters, or gift cards for their favorite indulgences. Learn what matters most to them and hook them up as often as possible. You will set yourself apart as a welcomed guest in their life, someone they will always be glad to hear from.

You are who you hang around. Find those who are both the most successful, yet most humble people you know. Study their patterns. If you do what they do, eventually, you will get what they have.

MAKE IT HAPPEN!

1. List the top five people you would love to have as a mentor:

Mentor's Name _____

What You Would Like To Learn

_____

Mentor's Name _____

What You Would Like To Learn

_____

Mentor's Name _____

What You Would Like To Learn

_____

Mentor's Name _____

What You Would Like To Learn

_____

Mentor's Name _____

What You Would Like To Learn

_____

2. Start a running list of people you need to thank. Keep this list in your phone or notebook. Start sending three thank you notes every week.

3. Listen to the interview on "Networking With Powerful People" in the *Get Off Your 'But' And Make It Happen Success Series*. These strategies found at www.GetAndStayMotivated.com will show you how easy it is to create instant rapport with Centers of Influence, make yourself look like a star, and stand out from your coworkers and competitors.

IDEAS AND ACTION ITEMS

_____

_____

_____

_____

_____

_____

_____

_____

_____

_____

IDEAS AND ACTION ITEMS

_____

_____

_____

_____

_____

_____

_____

_____

_____

_____

_____

Get Off Your 'BUT' And **PUT IN THE WORK**

"Stay active. Stay positive. Stay focused. Your time will come. Be ready."

-Jonathan Sprinkles

In the 1960's, Stanford University psychology researcher Michael Mischel conducted a groundbreaking study known as "The Stanford Marshmallow Study." He sat hungry four-year-olds in a room by themselves, offered them a marshmallow, and told them that if they could wait to eat it until he returned from running an errand, he would give them two marshmallows. As you would expect, most of the children gave into temptation. About one-third of them instantly grabbed the marshmallow and ate it. Some waited a little longer. Only one-third of the children were able to delay gratification for the 15 to 20 minutes he was outside the room. Twenty years later, Mischel's team discovered that in virtually every measurable statistic — including better academic performance, better health, higher incomes, even more successful marriages — the group of children with high self-discipline did better than those who yielded to temptation.

In today's "Download Generation" that demands everything *right now*, the concept of delayed gratification is nearly unheard of. I have been saying for years that, as a society, our collective impulsiveness and unwillingness to accept boundaries would come back to bite us. Now you know why.

People act as though now is the only time that matters. Tomorrow will have to take care of itself. We spend more and save less than at any other time in history. The Bureau of Economic Analysis reported that the national savings rate fell in 2005 to its lowest point since the Great Depression: negative 0.4 percent. Since then, it has come back slightly, but nowhere near the 1985 numbers, when it hit a record 11.1 percent. This exposes a widespread lack of future orientation, a lack of patience, and an overall lack of discipline. Currently, the national Retirement Confidence Survey reports that a stunning 70 percent of people surveyed say they are "a little" or "a lot" behind schedule in planning and saving for retirement. We are not putting money away like we used to. So much so, the United States government had to step in and attempt to stop the madness. Congress has designated October 18-24 as "National Save for Retirement" week. However, if there is a big sale that week, this may become the most uncelebrated holiday in history!

This era of consumerism is the epitome of the "latest and greatest" mentality. Microsoft runs the table in the software world, frequently releasing a new operating system that makes your current version seem obsolete. When Apple unveils an upgraded version of a product, people camp out in front of stores so they can be the first to brag to their friends that they have it, even if it is only slightly different from the version they already own. Air Jordan tennis shoes and John Madden Football video games rule the roost in their respective industries, commanding similar frenzies by their followers at the annual release of the next product in their series. It is unbelievable how we have trained ourselves to consider something "old" if it has been out for more than six months. Retailers have figured out how to use this buying habit to create annuities out of loyal followers who are dying to have this year's model at any cost.

Don't me wrong; I'm not pointing the finger. This is coming from a professed shoeaholic. Presently, I only have one kidney and half a lung because I sold the other parts for a pair of size 12 Magnanni's last month. I offered my pancreas for the matching belt, but they didn't have my size. Even when I don't plan to buy shoes that day, I'll still go to the shoe department "just to look." Don't you dare judge me! My covetousness over hot looking neckties is just as fierce. I have more ties than I have places to wear them. But they're *mine*, doggone it!

I am throwing myself under the bus because I want you to be clear that I am neither taking aim at businesses nor overzealous consumers. I whip out my wallet like a six-shooter when I see a killer sale. I get a rush from buying what I like…nay…love, just like you. However, it is time to shine a much-needed spotlight on what is happening to us as a result of our love/hate relationship with having something new right now versus saving for the future. All the numbers are saying the same thing—we are a very impatient people.

If you don't learn to "manage the marshmallows" in your life, you are stifling your future in many ways you may not suspect.

- You will prematurely quit your goals.
- You will be incapable of leading others.
- You will be in debt constantly, struggling because you're spending all your money instead of saving and investing.
- You will live with constant self-doubt, feeling powerless to change your circumstances.

Yes, it really is that deep. Personally, I believe that marshmallows are life's way of separating the haves from the have-nots. My über-successful colleague Larry Winget wisely quips that success is really a case of the "wills versus the will nots." **The "will not's" of this world are the ones who refuse to give up short-term pleasure so they can devote themselves to achieving long-term success.** It isn't that they can't put in the work, they just won't! What choices have you made recently?

- Work out or rest?
- Select a side salad or french fries?
- Save or shop?
- Pick up a book or the remote control?
- Bite your lip or "go off" when you're angry?

Marshmallows will always abound in your life. You need not ask, "Will I be tempted?" or even "How often?" You already know the answer: *yes, all the time!* You are constantly being tested to see how well you maintain your discipline and handle distractions. These are the greatest indicators for determining whether you will get from where you are to where you want to be.

Being totally transparent, I share with you that there are many bad decisions I've made that could have been good decisions had I taken more time—be it another minute or another month—to consider other options. The times I regret most were the byproduct of my getting caught up in the moment, having tunnel vision, and, consequently, failing to manage that marshmallow. With a little more perspective, I wouldn't have had to make that second phone call and say, "Hey, I didn't mean it like that" or "I'm sorry for speaking out of frustration." When I screw up, I often look back and think of 10 different alternatives that I didn't choose. Either I didn't think of them prior to the decision I made, or they weren't as attractive as the immediate gratification that Plan A brought me. As a member of the Download Generation, the seduction of *now* gets me, too.

Through my errors and learning lessons, I have discovered that "no" at the right time can actually help you, just as "yes" at the wrong time can hurt you. Sometimes, you don't immediately get what you want because the situation was meant to grow your patience as you wait for the Answer to become clear. Every day of the process, you become something greater than you were the day before. You take one step closer to your Answer, and it takes one step closer to you. Wisdom is knowing when to press in and when to sit back and trust the divine order of life. Knowing this, I have to often repeat to myself quietly, "Patience makes the grass grow," remembering that only weeds can grow overnight. Having to wait on your breakthrough is preparation, not a penalty. Something is being worked out inside you that will have you ready when your moment finally comes.

At the most practical level, "managing your marshmallows" is about controlling your moment instead of allowing the emotion of the moment to control you. You can only go in one direction at a time. You cannot move forward and build if you constantly have to go back and repair what you have damaged along the way. The time, creativity, and emotional energy that you could have invested in progress are spent on the phone cleaning up your mess. Damage control is draining, be it talking with your friends, getting yourself out of legal trouble, or trying to cover up your blunder so it doesn't get out to the public. The point is, had you known that all of this was going to be on the backend of the decision, surely, you wouldn't have chosen it in the first place.

While you may not be omniscient or psychic, the tool you do have at your disposal that will give you insight into your future is patience. It requires you to take the time to consider both the primary consequences (that which you expect to happen) and the secondary consequences (the hidden ones that you don't initially anticipate). When you have thought through your plan of action, you will find yourself moving forward with a greater level of confidence and assurance, even when there is no clear-cut correct answer. Making a tough decision is not nearly as stressful when you have gone through a mental checklist instead of selecting what is most appealing in the moment.

I have kept myself out of hot water a few times by repeatedly asking myself, "And then what?" That question forces me to look beyond the temporal satisfaction that the moment will bring and consider the impact that my choice will make on the relationship, my personal integrity, or my plan for the future. It can be something as simple as making a joke about someone or it can be more complex, such as choosing to partner with someone in business. Both cases have obvious and not-so-obvious ramifications for which I will be responsible, regardless of whether I saw them coming or not. Once it's done, it's done.

"And then what?" goes through my mind about 10,000 times every time I appear on television. I have seen too many people say something in jest or let a word flippantly slip off the tongue and then get fried because of it. Hollywood A-lister Jennifer Anniston once said the word "retard" on a talk show and you would have thought the world flipped on its head. She wasn't being malicious, but our culture has become so particular about political correctness (which is total baloney by the way), everyone gets offended when the approved words are not used. I'm sure she had to spend some big bucks making amends for her miscue, as have many other public figures for theirs. I tend to have strong opinions and do not like to bite my tongue. So, I have to be careful when I'm broadcasting before tens of millions of people because I will be held accountable for every word that comes out of my mouth. I don't intend to spend my retirement savings on public relations disaster recovery teams.

One incident that comes to mind is when I was invited to give commentary on a national TV program about an overweight girl who was asked not to sit on the front row of the audience at a taping of *American Idol*. The producers said it was because she had a large group with her and they couldn't accommodate that many seats. She said it was because she was overweight. At the time, it was a big story because the show is supposed to be about young people discovering their dreams, not about being put down because of their weight. Remember how I said I have strong opinions? This was one of those times. The backstory revealed that the young lady acknowledged that she was sensitive about her weight, which implied that she would be happier with herself at a smaller size. That's all I needed. I really can't stand when people play the victim role about things they can control. I was about to tear into both the show and the girl for being so darn sensitive. I was about to go on air and hit her with the line you see plastered across the back of this book—*If you don't like it, change it!* That would have made me look witty and confident. It would have put her in her place. It would have been great television, for sure. I had the marshmallow in my hand and was getting ready to pop it into my mouth.

But as I was writing my notes, I paused and asked myself the magic question, "And then what?" What if that were my daughter, struggling with self-esteem issues and already dealing with her peers picking on her and dozens of nasty messages on her Facebook page from people who had heard about the story and wanted to bring her down even further. What if I were the girl? What would I want to hear from a motivational speaker who could give me ten seconds of advice? I was that close to using my television segment as a bully pulpit at her expense. That is the exact opposite of everything I stand for. That is the reason I got into television in the first place, so people could hear intelligent opinions with a spiritual foundation. If I let her have it, then what?

Fortunately, this epiphany occurred moments before I got on air. Unfortunately, this epiphany happened only moments before I got on air. I mean, literally, two minutes prior. I didn't have much time to prepare a very eloquent statement. I felt like I stumbled through the entire segment, carefully avoiding the landmines such as using the wrong terminology about her weight. At the same time, I gave her and others in her situation my strong opinion on the matter. I will paraphrase what I said (or meant to say):

First of all, before we go jumping on American Idol, we have to remember there are three sides to every story: her side, their side, and the truth. If they did discriminate against her because of her weight, of course, they're wrong. If they had done that because she was Muslim and wore a hijab (head scarf), or because she was a minority, we'd all have a fit.

To the young lady, I have a word of advice: You can't let one event define you. What they allegedly said about you doesn't make you who you are. At this point, you have three choices. You can either wallow in victimhood, you can use this as motivation to finally lose the weight as you indicated you would like to, or you can use this as your platform to help other people who are being discriminated against.

You never know when you're going to be led to your purpose. Sometimes, even really bad times can produce great outcomes. You can turn a negative into a positive if you are determined to do so.

That was more like me. I told her the truth as I saw it without being condemning at the same time. I felt much better about this alternative than I would have had I taken the bait and used my time to blast either American Idol or the girl. The marshmallow was almost in my mouth; but I put it back down, proud that I won the battle—this time.

It is easier than you think to start your own marshmallow management system. Keep it simple. At least once a week, refrain from activities that have become habitual to you, such as eating (fasting is an excellent ritual practiced by millions of people), text messaging, social media, talking on the phone, shopping, or watching television. Your life will instantly get off autopilot when you make yourself break a pattern. For example, "No Texting Tuesday" will cause you to become aware of the many times you reach for your phone and get distracted by the many side conversations you have throughout your day. I promise you, you don't even realize how much time you're wasting unconsciously. Temporarily denying yourself puts space between the habitual impulse and the choice you make to engage it or not. You soon realize that you don't have to respond every time the text message alert dings. **Making the choice to intelligently respond instead of instinctively react is the foundation of sound decision making and reclaiming the power in your life.**

> **Making the choice to intelligently respond instead of instinctively react is the foundation of sound decision making and reclaiming the power in your life.**

Deciding to abstain from something you like in order to prepare yourself for something you love sends a loud message to your future. It says that you are stronger than your urges and mature enough to handle the responsibility of more influence, more opportunities, and more blessings. It is a form of addition by subtraction. It is never easy, but that's the point. It is still worth it. The key is to not think about how much it sucks to deny yourself what you want, but instead, to focus on the discipline you're teaching yourself through the process. It is never about what you're giving up; it is always about how you're growing.

What are you willing to give up in order to go higher?

MAKE IT HAPPEN!

Begin a new weekly discipline. "Meatless Mondays," "No Texting Tuesdays," or "Thank You Note Thursdays," are all examples of habits that will get you off autopilot and inspire you to be more intentional about how you live your life. Write the name(s) of your new weekly challenge(s) below.

_____

_____

_____

_____

_____

_____

_____

_____

_____

_____

_____

_____

IDEAS AND ACTION ITEMS

_____

_____

_____

_____

_____

_____

_____

_____

_____

_____

_____

_____

IDEAS AND ACTION ITEMS

_____

_____

_____

_____

_____

_____

_____

_____

_____

_____

_____

Get Off Your 'BUT' And **CLAIM YOUR BLESSINGS**

"Don't be so caught up in your plan that you miss God's will."

-Jonathan Sprinkles

I was beyond excited. After five years of silence, I was reemerging into the world of authorship. This book was, in my opinion, the best book anywhere on the planet for teaching emerging leaders the intangibles of leadership that nobody else was discussing. I had nailed it. It embodied my years of traveling the country, speaking, teaching, researching, coaching, and finding out what really works and what is just theory. Finally, I felt internally like I had arrived as a legitimate expert on my topic. I always wanted to write "the book." The one to which people who were talking in casual conversation would refer others as the go-to guide on this subject. My goal was to write not just a book, but a resource guide. It was to be so powerful, I could tell people, "Just read my book and all that you just asked me about will be answered and then some." I had poured my heart and soul into the project. This was more than paper and ink; it was my identity.

I dedicated the book to my mother. The inscription said, "This book I also dedicate to my mother, who taught me how to keep my emotional bank accounts in the black by investing in the greatest asset of all—other people." It was a surprise (I love creating "a-ha" moments for people). I just knew she was going to be floored by the gesture, as well as the wisdom shared in the contents that her baby boy had written.

She was the first person I mailed the book to when the boxes arrived. I sent it to her express delivery. Then I called her.

Me: Hey, Mom! How's it going?
Mom: Hey, Jon.
Me: (Filled with anticipation, unable to wait for her to bring it up) So, uh, did you get your copy of *Take Your Leadership to the Next Level*?
Mom: (Sounding hesitant) Uh…yeah.
Me: So…whatdaya think?
Pause.
Another pause.
Mom: Well, it's a great book Jon. But, did you get someone to read it over and edit it before you sent it off?
Me: WHAT? ARE YOU SERIOUS? Mom, I have slaved away at that book for months. I've read and re-read that darn book so many times, I can't stand to look at it anymore. I had a professional editor oversee the project. No book is perfect. I read a *New York Times* bestseller last week that I picked up at *your* house, and it had an error in it. People make mistakes. I'm not perfect. I don't care if there are mistakes in it. I don't care if you don't like it. I don't care because it was the best I could do. I can't believe I dedicated the book to you and that's all you can see. You know what, I've gotta go.

Conversation over.

For the next two months, I barely said a word to my mother. We didn't talk that often as it was, perhaps once every other week. After losing my father as a teen, I didn't like being close to people anymore. I kept everyone at bay emotionally. I could not and would not let anyone else in and risk being hurt like that again. Not even my mother. Previously we were relatively close. I still loved her as much as I could, but the relationship had reduced to being strictly "functional." Nevertheless, she was still my mother. Pardon—my mama! And that meant she was going to be the lady in my life whether I wanted it or not. She would call me (I never called her); we exchanged pleasantries; I pretended to be interested in whatever she was saying and searched for an excuse to get off the phone—quickly.

This carried on for a while. I avoided dealing with the root of the issue by denying that anything was wrong, although I clearly displayed in my attitude that something was wrong. I was hurting but didn't want to admit it to myself, let alone express it to her. The joy of my new book had deflated long ago. What I originally deemed as my masterpiece was now just a product that I was selling.

I remember the day it all hit me at once. It was as though I had been hit with a brick. I looked around and realized that nobody was there. Literally. It was just me. Something came over me and I realized the reality of my life. I was all alone. I had masterfully alienated myself from everyone by keeping them on the fringes of my life. The walls I erected to keep everyone out had left me trapped inside by myself. Mind you, this was occurring at a red-hot time in my career. I was speaking and teaching all over the country. This happened only months before I was voted National Speaker of the Year. Outwardly, things could not have been better. But all the large speaking fees in the world couldn't pay for what I needed most: a friend.

My heart began racing. I had shortness of breath. This must have been what Ebenezer Scrooge went through in *A Christmas Carol* when he was being visited by the Ghosts of Christmas Past and Future. I sat there, nearly in tears, realizing what a mess I had made of my life and what a stupid decision I had made about my mother.

"You fool," I said to myself. "She's all you've got. You don't have a father; you don't have any grandparents. Your mother is getting up in age. Once she goes, *that's it!* If she died today, your last memory of her would be of this argument. Is that what you want? Are you going to punish her for the rest of her life over—a book?"

I couldn't believe I had been so careless. I was beyond disappointed; I was embarrassed. That evening, on my drive to Bible study, I called her.

Me: Mom?
Mom: Yes.
Me: Mom, I know I've been acting funny for the past couple months. It all goes back to the conversation we had about the book. I was really hurt because you were so critical about it and I was super-sensitive to your comments. I retreated and didn't want to talk to you anymore. That was wrong. I'm sorry, Mom.
Mom: Jon, you are my son. I know you. I have known you since before you were born. I knew something was wrong. I knew why it was wrong. I, too, realized that I did the wrong thing by criticizing your book instead of congratulating you for your accomplishment. And I'm sorry.

That was the end of the conversation. It was two months in the making; five minutes in the resolution. I could not believe it was so easy. It was one of the toughest conversations I have ever had, but I am so glad it happened. I grew exponentially through that process. Our relationship has grown as well. I now call her every Sunday, regardless of where I am in the country. And we always close the call by saying, "I love you."

Some may find it ironic that the chapter entitled "Get Off Your 'But' And **CLAIM YOUR BLESSINGS**" is headlined by a message on forgiveness. Before I went through that experience, I would have, too. You may see no correlation between the blessings you want to receive and the mercy you have to give. The two are mutually exclusive, right?

Picture this.

Imagine yourself running a marathon. Just before you take off, an official at the starting point hands you a vest with pockets and instructs you to put it on. "What's this for?" you ask. "You'll see," she says.

Every few blocks, an onlooker emerges from the crowd and places a stone in one of the pockets. It seems odd; but because the stones aren't that heavy, it's no big deal and you press on. However, as your pockets begin to fill, the weight of your vest becomes more evident. You feel yourself becoming fatigued uncommonly fast and your pace decreases to half its original speed. Eventually, you wear down to a jog, then a slow trot, until you are finally walking.

You look back and realize you haven't traveled nearly as far as you thought you had. You can't remember the last time you became this tired in such a short amount of time. Of course, the collection of stones in your vest is the culprit.

"These darn things have ruined my race," you yell at the top of your voice in frustration. You reach deep into one of the pockets, ready to throw them as far as your strength will allow. You dig until you find a big one, one that will travel far and, you hope, do some damage upon impact. You're that mad. You clinch the rock tightly and prepare yourself to hurl it high and far. But just before you cock your hand, you catch something out of the corner of your eye. Something is written on the stone.

It says, "CHEATER."

You are mortified. Intuitively you know that this word isn't aimed at you, but is a direct quote from a conversation you recently had about a former spouse of years ago. You went on and on about their infidelity like you had just found out that day. You came up with every negative word in the book to describe them. "Cheater" was the nicest of the words you used.

You drop that rock, curious, and begin searching your pockets to see if there is anything written on the others. To your amazement, there are words written on all of them!

"Stupid."
"Ugly."
"You're such a loser."
"Abuse."
"Divorcee."
"Fear of abandonment."
"People pleasing."
"Bankruptcy."
"Parent's death."
"Loneliness."
"Absentee father."
"Control issues."
"Impatience."
"You don't finish anything."

As you dump your pockets, the list goes on, with each word speaking to different incidents in your life. Written on several of them are even names of people you can't stand the thought of. It doesn't take long for you to realize that these are more than just randomly-selected stones; they are your issues.

Of all our many choices in life, the greatest spiritual test we will confront is choosing to forgive. Anyone can be religious. Only spiritual people can forgive. The act of releasing the rocks in our life is completely counterintuitive. Intellectually, it doesn't make sense. But spiritually, it is a requirement.

Personally, I have to fight myself not to be a grudge-holder. When someone does me wrong, my initial instinct is to go back to that place in my life that I nurtured as a teen. When my father died, I learned how to emotionally cut people off completely. That was my way of dealing with things—"Just go away and I'll erase any memory of your ever being here." It is easy and it is efficient. But it isn't godly. And it isn't even accurate. The next time I would see the person, feelings of anger that were dormant would reemerge. This exposed the truth about the failure of my coping mechanism. I hadn't dealt with the emotions, I had just taught them to behave.

My experiences of winning and losing battles with reconciliation have taught me a lot about how embracing the opportunity to forgive can enhance your life.

I HAVE LEARNED: Forgiving is a wealth strategy.

Wealth? Yes, wealth. Studies have concluded repeatedly that those who quickly resolve interpersonal conflicts live more successful lives. They think more clearly, have more energy, are more creative, achieve their goals more quickly, and do significantly better professionally. If you understand the phrase *your wealth is in your health,* you understand why. Prolonged anger takes a toll on your body and reduces your capacity to achieve. When you're sick, you can't work. Unresolved emotional issues weaken your immune system, leaving you susceptible to short- or long-term illnesses and diseases. It has been well-documented that a distressed psychological state, over time, can weaken the immune system and has been linked to cancer, viruses, neurological diseases, and various breakdowns of the autoimmune system. Hands that are full of rocks cannot hold on to blessings.

I HAVE LEARNED: What goes around, comes around.

The most humbling experience you can have is being on your knees, asking for forgiveness, and being reminded of someone you have yet to let go of. Isn't it crazy how easily we can ask for forgiveness for our bad decisions but can't seem to do the same for others? This is why it says that God's ways are not our ways. I don't care what religious book you read, none of the featured higher powers has a policy that says, "Don't you let that jive turkey off the hook!" God isn't petty; we are. But the requirement is still the same. We cannot truly receive forgiveness for our mistakes if we continue to hold other people's mistakes over their heads.

In my faith, grace and mercy are the cornerstones of a relationship with God. Grace is giving you what you don't deserve. Mercy is not giving you something you do. This is why God can't fully utilize people with anger in their hearts. We can't receive grace, but dish out revenge. It doesn't work that way. People who try to circumvent the system end up being a nightmare to deal with. God's blessings become misappropriated, used as weapons against people instead of tools to serve them. Failure to pass along the mercy we've been given blocks the blessings and reduces our godly potential.

I HAVE LEARNED: Forgiveness frees.

It may be wise to not deal with them, but it is not wise to not forgive them. Harboring resentment keeps that person from exiting your life. It is like kicking someone out of your house but leaving the porch light on and the door unlocked. I used to believe that pardoning people was a sign of weakness. It was for people who didn't have the backbone to stand up for themselves. I saw it as my only source of strength to get back at someone who, I felt, wronged me. Little did I know, they weren't even thinking about me anymore! I was going to bed frustrated, with my face all twisted up, envisioning all the bad things I wanted to happen to them, and they were at home sleeping like a baby. When I held on to my anger, they got me twice!

All of this changed when I adopted a philosophy from people who also have been deeply wounded. Oprah Winfrey, for one, lived with the emotional scars left by a history of sexual abuse from a family member. Through her journey from pain to forgiveness, she had to grow into giving herself permission to let go. She now understands that "Forgiving doesn't mean you're telling them it's okay. It means you're telling them they won't have control over your life." My former belief that forgiveness weakens you was dead wrong. My conviction about punishing people by remaining angry was equally incorrect. My sister Caryn shared with me an insight that turned my thinking around. She said, "Forgiving people doesn't let them off the hook; it gets you off theirs." I am now clear that being intentional about letting go is an act of strength and maturity. Most importantly it allows you to reclaim your power and regain what the situation took from you in the first place—your peace. When you forgive someone, you are liberated. And when you apologize, you get promoted.

Comedian and author Steve Harvey shared a personal story that also has reshaped my philosophy on this topic. After a very public fallout with a former colleague, Steve was having dinner with Judge Greg Mathis (from "The Judge Mathis Show") and shared with him the raw emotions he was dealing with. One side of him was devastated; another wanted revenge. Judge Mathis turned his shoulders square to Steve, looked at him eye-to-eye and said, "Steve, you can't be big and small at the same time." Judge Mathis urged Steve to make a choice about who he wanted to be. He could choose to live out of his lower nature that fights people or he could be his higher self that builds empires. Getting even meant going backward.

> **In life, lessons are taught through interactions with people, experience-by-experience.**

At a charity event we were both attending, Terrance Jenkins (known as "Terrance J" on BET's "106th and Park") said, "Life is all about energy." Those five words resonated with me at my core. Your life is the sum total of where you choose to expend your energy. Use this as your litmus test to decide *is this really worth it?* "Worth it" does not mean it will make you feel better temporarily. "Worth it" means knowing that you're choosing to reduce your supply of goal-achieving, life-improving, vision-building energy for the day and redirect it toward dragging someone else down. Stop for a second and ask yourself, "What do I intend to accomplish?" Will giving that energy away get you down the road to your goals any faster or does it leave both of you stalled on the side? A Buddhist philosopher put it best, "There are no good decisions. There are no bad decisions. There are only decisions. But the way you deal with your decisions determines the person you become."

I HAVE LEARNED: People are our teachers.

Every experience with a person is a learning experience…if we choose to accept the lesson. They teach you what you need to learn so you can know what you need to know so you can become what you are supposed to be. In school, lessons are taught in a book, chapter-by-chapter. **In life, lessons are taught through interactions**

with people, experience-by-experience. The event for which you have to forgive someone wasn't about him or her; it was about you.

There are no accidents in this world. Everything happens for a reason. That person was your teacher who was being used, even unknowingly, to bring you a lesson that you needed to get in order to prepare you for your next level. Their selfishness taught you to be unselfish. Their immaturity taught you to grow up quickly. Their cheating taught you to value faithfulness. Their abuse taught you to value those who love unconditionally.

Once again, you would never have signed up for the pain, but when you look back and consider the many lessons that you got from the process, it makes sense.

I HAVE LEARNED: The longer you wait, the stronger it becomes.

The Internet has made it possible for everyone to have a voice. That is awesome. The not-so-awesome part about it is that not everyone chooses to use their voice positively.

As I embarked upon my media career, I began to prepare myself to have very thick skin. And I did so in an unconventional manner. I read the comments at the end of articles and learned an invaluable lesson: no matter how you put it or what your intention was, someone will always be offended. Someone will find fault with everything you do. Everything! Especially because the Internet affords us the opportunity to unleash vitriolic tirades while remaining anonymous, people say whatever the heck they want without consequence. I've read comments that people would *never* say to someone's face, but they can talk big noise while hiding behind a keyboard.

People are going to talk trash. People are going to try to get under your skin. They will spin your good deeds into making you look bad. So? Even my program evaluations reflect this. Ninety-nine people will say, "You rock!" And there's always that one person who says, "You suck!" So what? Let it go and move on. The longer you hold on to negative emotions, the stronger they become.

Their actions reflect their mentality.

Conversely, when you learn the art of quickly processing and discarding negative feelings, they don't have time to multiply and grow. I have had to learn to see people's opinions as just that—opinions. Some are complimentary; some are demeaning. They're still only opinions. Rudyard Kipling, in his poem "If," said, "If you can meet with triumph and disaster and treat those two imposters just the same." Both sides of the opinion poll are only as true as you allow them to be.

Moreover, the way people refer to you reveals more about them than it does about you. Don't waste your time stewing in your mind over questions such as, "Why did he say that? What makes her think this about me?" You don't have the power to change people's perceptions of you. You will never know a person's true motivations for saying the things they do. Neither is it your business! All you can do is "do you" and let them eventually come around…or not. You have to let people be where they are. **Their actions reflect their mentality.** That's on them, not on you.

Martial arts master Bruce Lee said, "The best way to defeat an enemy is to not have one in the first place." For you, the point is to avoid becoming embroiled in emotion by not letting yourself go there in the first place. Decide to receive the feedback of only a few key people whose opinions you trust. Everyone else gets the same pre-canned response, "Thank you. God bless you." And be done.

After all this reflection on the topic of forgiving and apologizing, I realize I have a few calls to make and letters to write. Be sure to ask me how it went.

I suppose you may, as well. On the next page, write the names of people you need to reach out to. As you cross each name off your list, do a short celebration, knowing that you are one step closer to emptying your rocks once-and-for-all.

Also, write the names of some people who came to your mind as you read this chapter. Include both those you need to forgive and those to whom you feel compelled to apologize. **Now is the time. Free yourself!**

MAKE IT HAPPEN!

While you are in the moment, create a list of people who came to mind as you read this chapter. Write a letter or make a phone call to each of the people below, telling them how you feel.

People I Need To Release By Forgiveness:

_____

_____

_____

_____

_____

People I Need To Release By Apologizing:

_____

_____

_____

_____

_____

IDEAS AND ACTION ITEMS

_____

_____

_____

_____

_____

_____

_____

_____

_____

_____

_____

IDEAS AND ACTION ITEMS

Get Off Your 'But' And **MAKE IT HAPPEN**

JONATHAN SPRINKLES

EPILOGUE

A recent report released by the Jenkins Group stated that 57 percent of books are not read to completion. Statistically speaking, I could be wasting my time by boohooing and sharing anything too sentimental right now because there is a great chance I'm talking to myself. I could reveal my PIN number right now and most people would never find out! Just jokes.

Getting to this point has been a labor of love. You would never know this, but I rewrote this book four-and-a-half times before it got to the finished product. It was originally intended to be something completely different than what you have in your hands. The first time I thought I was "finished," something clicked inside. I erased what I had previously written. Then, floods of new information began to flow through me.

Literally, I would start writing on a topic that I had no intention of discussing, and the right words and stories would just "come to me." If you have ever experienced anything like this, you know what I'm talking about. I let my fingers do the talking.

When I became open to moving aside my own agenda and allowing these ideas to pour out through me, a stream of consciousness flowed time and time again. It quickly became apparent to me that this book isn't about me or my so-called wisdom. It is a special collection of messages intended to give you exactly what you need to help you connect with a bigger version of what you already are.

This project is much greater than the messenger. I am just honored to be the one chosen to deliver it to you.

In closing, my parting message to you is simple.

I believe there is something insanely beautiful about you. I believe you haven't even seen your best days yet. I believe you are the answer to someone's prayers. I believe God knew exactly what He was doing when He made you exactly how you are at exactly the perfect time. I believe there is a power at work in you that is greater and more profound than you ever imagined. I believe you were born not just to make money, make headlines, or make people laugh, but to make a small difference in the life of everyone you encounter. I believe history has a place with your name on it, if you choose to devote yourself to your gift. I believe your greatness will be remembered by the way you do ordinary things extraordinarily well.

I believe that you can become anything you want if you are willing to invest the time to learn. I believe that the moment you decide to show up and live your purpose, resources will manifest that have been lying dormant all along, waiting for you to arrive. I believe obedience, discipline, and faith will slay any giant that stands in your way. I believe there are no limits for you—none. I believe you can dream big, even in small places. I believe there are two versions of your life: a large one and a small one. I believe the large one is so amazing it would intimidate someone else, but fits you perfectly—because it's yours. I believe that you can do it. I believe you know you can, too. I believe it's time. I believe it's your time. I believe in you.

Make it happen.

Te amo,

JONATHAN SPRINKLES

MEET JONATHAN SPRINKLES

WINNER
Mentor Of The Year
Eastman Kodak
Disney Dreamer's Academy

WINNER
Speaker Of The Year
APCA

WINNER
40 Under 40
Houston Business Journal

WINNER
Pinnacle Award
HCCC

"Your Connection Coach," Jonathan Sprinkles, delivers straight talk, 'sprinkled' with laughs. He is a television commentator, featured columnist, author, and a leading authority on personal development strategies for leaders and achievers.

Jonathan's tips on connecting in business and in relationships have been featured in:

Forbes.com	**ABC**
Glamour.com	**Fox News**
The Huffington Post	**Headline News**
Essence.com	**USA Today**

For over a decade, organizations like yours have trusted Jonathan to provide a high-energy, high-results message on **Motivation, Leadership, Communication, Change, and Sales.**

Here's why: he's funny; his energy keeps audiences fully engaged; he has a gift for **inspiring people** to **achieve at a higher level**; and most importantly, **his strategies work.** Throughout his career, Jonathan has been consistently recognized as a leading authority in helping people and organizations create a culture in which they are more connected with each other and with the organization's vision. Jonathan's techniques and teaching style come from experience. Having faced many of the same personal, financial, and organizational challenges your audience has endured, Jonathan "gets it." He knows what looks good on paper versus what really works in the real world. Because he has been there, he speaks to the intangibles that finally connect the dots between theory and implementation. He uses elements of his personal journey from failure and embarrassment to becoming a top-rated expert in his field to remind his audiences to **aim high and reject excuses**.

Jonathan Sprinkles' message has made him a favorite at banquets, conventions, and training events. Jonathan's company, Sprinklisms, Inc., was recently honored as the **Pinnacle Award Winner** for excellence in business. Jonathan was voted *Houston Business Journal's "40 Under 40"* for being one of the top entrepreneurs in America's fourth largest city. He has also been voted **National Speaker of the Year** (APCA), **Marketer of the Year** (JMI), and **Mentor of the Year** (Disney/Eastman Kodak).

> **"My mission is to equip people to connect with a bigger version of their lives."**

Jonathan's passion for helping people perform at their best stems from the agony that he felt when he lost his father to cancer at the age of 15. Attempting to mask the pain, he gave into peer pressure and the low expectations that surround many African-American men. However, Jonathan's spirit wouldn't allow him to stay down. Refusing to settle for life's second best, he graduated college from the fourth-ranked marketing program in the country. At graduation, he was awarded the two highest leadership designations given to any student out of an enrollment of over 53,000.

After college, Jonathan enjoyed a thriving career as a top salesman at Dell, Inc. Jonathan was hand-picked by senior management to join an elite group of Senior Account Managers who were responsible for acquiring new business in the fastest-growing segment of the company. Because of the leadership, customer service, and team-building skills he developed within a high-stakes sales environment, Jonathan was bestowed with the coveted title of "Significant Achiever" among a pool of 400 of the corporation's best sales reps.

Jonathan opted out of the fast-track in his corporate position to launch his own company and live his mission to equip people to connect with bigger lives. His high-energy presentations go against the grain of traditional thinking that is rooted in myths that sound good but don't work in today's marketplace.

After just a few minutes with Jonathan, his quick wit and down-home style of "teaching beautiful people to act like it" will make you feel like you've known him your entire life. Jonathan Sprinkles' life is one that we can all celebrate as proof that success isn't about where you start, but where you choose to finish!

TAKE THE NEXT STEP IN CREATING A 'KICK-BUT' CAREER AND LIFE.

Additional Resources For Your Immediate Success

STEP 1 – Get Off Your 'BUT' & MAKE IT HAPPEN – ENHANCED AUDIOBOOK [Information]
Enjoy a one-on-one coaching and mentorship experience with Jonathan as he reads this book to you. Energize your daily drive, exercise routine, or personal time.

STEP 2 – Get Off Your 'BUT' & MAKE IT HAPPEN – ACTION GUIDE
[Implementation]
Jonathan walks you step-by-step through each phase of your goals. Fill in the blanks, write your vision, and plan your next big move. Create your own customized success plan that can't fail!

STEP 3 – Get Off Your 'BUT' & MAKE IT HAPPEN – DAILY MOTIVATOR [Inspiration]
Stay on track by reading a special-edition compilation of additional, powerful quotes from Jonathan Sprinkles on each chapter of this book.

www.GetAndStayMotivated.com

ENTER COUPON CODE: **OFFYOURBUT** AND
BUY 1, GET 1 50% OFF!*
Any item of equal or lesser value.

Request Jonathan Sprinkles For Your Next Event

For over a decade, organizations like yours have trusted Jonathan Sprinkles to deliver his powerful message to audiences of all sizes. If you want higher meeting evaluations and results that last long after the meeting ends, Jonathan is your man.

Visit the "Request Jonathan" page at
www.JSprinkles.com

twitter: @jsprinkles

facebook: @jsprinklesfans